DEREK BELL

My Racing Life

Derek Bell with Alan Henry

Patrick Stephens

Front endpaper *The moment of victory at Le Mans – for the fifth time – in 1987. A wonderfully atmospheric shot as the winning Porsche 962 slows to a halt in front of the pits.*

Rear endpaper *On the banking at Daytona in 1987 – and en route in the Löwenbräu Porsche 962 to a second straight victory in the US 24-hour classic.*

First published in 1988

British Library Cataloguing in Publication Data

Bell, Derek
    My racing life.
    1. Racing cars. Racing. Bell, Derek
    I. Title   II. Henry, Alan, *1947 –*
    796.7′2′0924

    ISBN 1-85260-107-8

*Patrick Stephens Limited is part of the
Thorsons Publishing Group, Wellingborough,
Northamptonshire NN8 2RQ, England.*

Printed by Butler & Tanner Limited, Frome, Somerset

10 9 8 7 6 5 4 3 2 1

Contents

Acknowledgements

THERE are countless people who have helped to make this book possible in a very short time and to whom my thanks are due. They include Trudy Wybrott, for her fast, efficient and accurate typing of final manuscript; Steven Tee, Malcolm Bryan and Jeremy Shaw, for chasing and organizing photographs from all over the world in double-quick time; Mick Earle, of Onyx Racing, for use of his FAX facilities; Pam Bell, for her considerate hospitality while Derek and I spent hours talking; Justin Bell, for providing a high-speed messenger service at a time when he was busy trying to sort out his own racing plans for a new season; and to Planners International for help and guidance.

No book is complete without illustrations and I must give particular thanks to the following photographers and sources, whose work appears here: Harold Barker, Malcolm Bryan, Craig Fischer, *France Soir*, Jerry B. Howard and Associates, LAT Photographic, T. C. March, Michael Marchant, *Motor*, Rothmans, Evan Selwyn-Smith, Gerry Stream, Colin Taylor, Les Thacker, *The Times*, Derek Whitby and Peter Wilson. My thanks, also, to Derek himself, for letting me plunder his personal collection of photographs.

Alan Henry
Tillingham

Author's introduction

I SUPPOSE this book amounts to a whirlwind trip for readers down memory lane, with me escorting them through some of the trials, tribulations, joys and successes produced by almost a quarter-century behind the wheel of a whole kaleidoscope of different racing cars.

That time has shot by unbelievably quickly. It seems only yesterday that I was setting out, full of optimism, to forge myself a Grand Prix career, yet here I am today with the vast majority of my success produced, not from single-seaters, but from sports cars in what have predominantly been long-distance races.

To offer thanks to all those who have helped, or featured, in this book would require a supplement which would probably be as long again. But significant personalities who immediately come to mind obviously include my stepfather Bernard Hender – 'The Colonel' – without whom I would never have got started in serious single-seater racing; Tom Wheatcroft, who rescued my fortunes at a crucial moment in 1970; and perhaps most of all my family – Pam, Justin and Melanie – who have put up with having a husband and father who was seldom home when they wanted him to be over the past 20 years.

This book came about in record time thanks to the collaboration of Darryl Reach and his team at PSL, my business manager David Mills and co-author Alan Henry who sat, patiently and amused, through what amounted to several verbal Le Mans races before sorting out the narrative into some kind of presentable order.

I first got to know Alan Henry in 1970 when he was a wet-behind-the-ears new boy covering my Formula 2 exploits with the Wheatcroft Brabham. Although our career paths diverged considerably thereafter, we always got on well and the moment I saw his outline synopsis I realized he would be ideal to work with me on my book. I well recall one occasion in the pit lane at Brands Hatch in 1983 when an endurance race was being held a week prior to the Grand Prix of Europe. Alan turned up in the pits and I admonished him rather acidly, saying, 'Haven't you turned up a week too early?' – the implication being that he was one of these elitist F1 people. The look on his face suggested that I'd touched a raw nerve! But we have had some enormously enjoyable days together producing this book and I hope he now has a slightly deeper insight into sports car racing than perhaps he did before he started.

I can only sum up my racing career so far with the words that I regularly use when I am giving an after-dinner speech on the subject: 'I've been doing something which is my hobby, my career and my business all rolled into one. I've travelled the world, met interesting people, driven lots of good cars – and been paid for it.

'Haven't I been lucky!'

Derek Bell
Pagham

Chapter 1

Early successes
and setbacks

I T WAS in the summer of 1968, I suppose, that I really began to
think I could make it to the top in motor racing. I had always been
passionately single-minded about having a crack at the World Championship, ever since I started with a Lotus Seven back in 1964, but I
always had it in the back of my mind that my cars were better than
my rivals'. I was never bullishly self-confident in any way, apart from
those few occasions in every racing driver's career when everything
clicks and you realize that, in that car, in that mood, on that day,
nobody is going to beat you.

There are perhaps a handful of occasions in your life when you just
know that you are better than the opposition. In my case I used to
feel that if I drove well enough on the day, then I might produce a
strong result. But basically I never felt terribly confident in my own
ability. But I just knew, for example, that I was going to win Le Mans
in 1981. I don't know why, but I just sensed it. It was the same in
1967 when I won the big late-season F3 race at Oulton Park in the
Felday Brabham BT21, and again at Barcelona in 1970 when I beat
Fittipaldi and the field to win in my Formula 2 Brabham BT30.

Of course, some of my contemporaries may say, 'Quite right,
those were the only times in your career when you *were* any bloody
good!' but I think they will all recognize the sort of situation I'm
referring to. You often get into a car at the start of a race knowing
that the machine is good enough, but you're not always certain that
you can provide the added ingredient to guarantee success on the
day.

Anyway, by 1968 things were looking good. I had served my
motor racing apprenticeship with three years in Formula 3 and now I
was tackling Formula 2 in my own Brabham BT23C, operated and
prepared from our own workshops down at my family home, Church

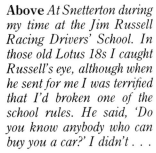

Above *At Snetterton during my time at the Jim Russell Racing Drivers' School. In those old Lotus 18s I caught Russell's eye, although when he sent for me I was terrified that I'd broken one of the school rules. He said, 'Do you know anybody who can buy you a car?' I didn't . . .*

Above right *Goodwood, March 1965: in amongst a club Formula 3 grid with my Lotus 31-BMC which we soon re-engined with a home-brewed Ford unit. It was my first step in a single-seater career that would take me to the cockpit of a Formula 1 Ferrari – briefly – three years later.*

Farm, at Pagham, on the Sussex coast. In those days the career path of an aspiring Grand Prix star was simple and straightforward. It was Formula 3, Formula 2 and Formula 1. More importantly, Formula 2 was still regularly contested by the established top Formula 1 drivers. You could go out in your private Lotus or Brabham, as I did, and get an accurate measure of your own talent in a straight fight with Graham Hill, Jochen Rindt or Jackie Stewart. It was a tremendously valuable experience.

Prior to Formula 2, I had spent three years in Formula 3, supported by my stepfather, Bernard Hender, known to all and sundry as 'The Colonel'. We'll be coming back to him in more detail later in the book, but it's right that I should record his contribution to my career at this early stage. He was quite the most remarkable benefactor any young driver could have had.

At the end of 1964 we sold my Lotus Seven and we made plans to move into Formula 3, using an elderly Lotus 31 fitted with a BMC engine. Prepared by John Upton at home and entered under the Church Farm Racing banner, which sounded more impressive than simply D. Bell, I was third first time out at the Boxing Day Mallory Park meeting and we soon swapped the BMC engine for a Ford.

Throughout 1965 I enjoyed some success in club racing and by the end of the year it was decided that I should have a new car for the following season. Rightly or wrongly, we decided to buy another Lotus, and a new type 41 was brought down to Goodwood for Piers Courage, Jonathan Williams and Peter Gethin to try their hand in. I got invited along because I lived nearby and had already been in touch with the factory about the possibility of buying one of these cars. I ended up second fastest to Piers and we cemented the deal to buy a 41.

I had all manner of shunts and crashes all over the Continent the following summer. It was a terrible year and I suppose I learned a lot

The scene is Brands Hatch, the car Cuff Miller's Marcos which I also drove occasionally throughout 1965. Clearways was never such hard work, surely?

from it, although I really didn't have much of a clue how to set up a single-seater racing car, and neither did my mechanic.

By the end of the year we had the biggest load of spare parts you've ever seen in your life, propped up in the corner of the workshop. I seemed to be crashing it every weekend. I rolled it into a ball, was upside down at Enna, and went through between two trees at Pau and took all the wheels off, shooting out the other side sitting in what felt like a cigar tube.

The Colonel was paying for all this, yet he never raised an eyebrow or said a word. Bearing in mind the way I went on at my son Justin if he even so much as tapped a wall in his Formula Ford car, I think the Old Man was just unbelievable. Anyway, by the end of the

Wrong choice! Adjusting my goggles in the cockpit of a works Lotus 41, which had been brought down to Goodwood for several drivers to test towards the end of 1965. Unwisely, I opted to buy one for the 1966 season, which turned out to be a mistake. I should have got my hands on a Brabham. On the right, in the cap, is Peter Warr, F1 Lotus team manager in the 1980s.

Above *Early street machine. I was lucky enough to enjoy this second-hand Jaguar E-type as my regular road machine for several years.*

Below *Continental campaign. Wrestling the Lotus round the Cascais road circuit, in Portugal, during that long, frustrating summer of '66 which saw the poor Lotus pretty badly bashed about!*

1966 season I was beginning to get the hang of it and took a fifth place at Albi and one or two other top-six finishes.

However, I wasn't too keen to continue with a Lotus in 1967. I'd had enough of the factory ringing me up on a Monday asking, 'Where did the rear wheel go this weekend? And which one was it? Oh yes, we had hub troubles like that with the works cars . . .' and so on.

The Colonel was paying for all this, yet he never raised an eyebrow.

I had been offered drives with de Sanctis and BWA in Italy and was due to fly down for some testing in November when I met Peter Westbury while testing at Brands Hatch. Peter had made a name for himself in hill-climb circles and was anxious to tackle Formula 3 very seriously. So, after some debate, we agreed that we would join up and field a team of three Brabham BT21s in 1967 with Peter, me and Mac Daghorn as the drivers. They were to be run from Peter's base at Felday Engineering, near Dorking in Surrey.

I suppose this was the year when I really began to grab some attention and make the headlines in the motor racing press. Second at Barcelona, third at Monaco, a win at Zolder, then second again at Albi, by only half a length from Henri Pescarolo in the Matra who was regarded as France's most promising rising star of the moment. At the end of the year I took the second Grovewood Award behind Alan Rollinson, sat down and considered my future. What was I going to do now?

Above *Works versus privateer! Chasing Jack Oliver's Charles Lucas/Team Lotus factory-assisted 41 round Becketts in the damp, late 1966. We swapped places several times during this battle, but eventually I finished third, both of us beaten by David Cole's Brabham.*

Below *Silverstone again, this time in the 41 dicing with Peter Gethin's Brabham. Five years later he and I both had test drives for the JW/Gulf Porsche team at Goodwood, after which I got the vacant seat co-driving with Jo Siffert.*

Right choice! At the end of 1966 we ordered a Brabham BT21 for the following season, when it was run by Peter Westbury's Felday outfit. Here I am ahead of Tony Lanfranchi's similar machine on the way to a maiden victory in the car at the 1966 Boxing Day Brands Hatch meeting.

I had been offered a drive in the works Chevron team run by Chris Williams, but if I'd stayed on for a fourth year in Formula 3 I would have been obliged to do even better. If I *had* done better, then people would have said, 'So he damn' well should . . .' If I'd only done as well, they would say, 'So what?' And, worst of all, if I hadn't done as well, it would have been a case of, 'There you are, it was a flash in the pan in 1967 . . .'

There was no question about it. I had to move up to Formula 2 in 1968. The previous year I had watched Robin Widdows graduate into F2 and I knew I was as good as Widz. He'd raised his own finance, established the Witley Racing Syndicate, and gone and done his own thing with a private Brabham. I figured from my experience with the Felday team that the Brabham was clearly the right way to go.

Of course, the next problem was establishing how on earth I was going to pay for a project like this. By the time we'd got to the end of 1967, The Colonel had paid for three years of my motor racing, so it seemed impossible that he would be able to help any further. He just had to say, 'Right, Derek, that's it, I'm out. I've spent enough money, I've enjoyed it all, but I think you're on your own from here on in'.

But he was still remarkably generous and told me I could have the F3 car and all the bits and pieces that went with it, to put towards my next project. I think the only proviso was that I didn't go buying myself an E-type Jaguar to cruise round the Bognor coffee bars!

So I sold the F3 Brabham. We didn't have a transporter, because that had been provided by the Felday team, so I managed to raise about three thousand quid altogether. That wasn't going to stretch very far. A new Brabham BT23C chassis was £2,500. We needed a couple of Cosworth FVA engines at £2,500 a time and, with a thousand pounds' worth of gear ratios and various other odds and ends, the whole budget worked out to about ten thousand pounds. Where did we get that from?

I got a reply from Avis who enclosed a little badge saying 'We Try Harder'.

By this stage I think the Old Man had pretty well decided that I wasn't going to be a farmer, so I spent most of my waking hours in that little office at Church Farm writing what seemed at the time like half a million letters to potential sponsors. The only positive response I got was a reply from Avis who enclosed a little badge saying 'We Try Harder'. That was the only encouragement I received.

Anyway, I decided it had to be a case of in for a penny, in for a pound. I put a £500 deposit on the Brabham, £500 down for each of the engines and £500 down on a truck. So, I was left with £500 with which to purchase another eight grand's worth of equipment. It didn't really add up terribly well!

At this point the Old Man realized that I was trying damned hard to get the show on the road. My mechanic, Ray Wardell, had been sent off to Brabhams to build the car and then went on to Cosworth in order to learn about the engines we had ordered . . . and we had no way of paying for the whole bang shoot!

Then the Old Man came to my rescue again. He said, 'I can see we're going to have to do it again . . .' and we went off down to the good old Nat West in Bognor, spoke to the manager and borrowed ten thousand pounds!

So off we went. I tested a few times at Goodwood just to get the hang of it, then we trailed all the way down to Barcelona only to miss the race after a valve broke in practice. Our second engine hadn't been delivered by that stage, so there was nothing to do but come home again.

I was totally green to the whole business, but I knew we had to be meticulously organized to have any chance of success and our little team really did very well. The BT23C was a great little car, a true classic, and everything seemed right. But our second outing was to Hockenheim, a race which had quite a profound effect on me. It was the one in which Jimmy Clark was killed.

It was the first time I'd ever met him. We were all staying at the Hotel Luxhof, in Speyer, just a few miles from the track. Graham Hill was there too, and I'll never forget sitting down to have tea on the Saturday afternoon with him and Jimmy. Me, still wet behind the

Tragic weekend. At the wheel of the Church Farm Racing F2 Brabham BT23C, swinging through the right-hander into the stadium at Hockenheim, 6 April 1968. In the following day's race, Jim Clark crashed to his death at the wheel of his works Lotus.

ears, sitting there with two of my great heroes!

It had been raining all weekend and, when we had breakfast together on the Sunday morning, Jimmy said, 'Don't get too close behind me when you come up to lap me because my car is cutting out intermittently . . .'

I thought, 'This is my idol saying *when you come up to lap me,*' and it was a bit difficult to take in. But I'd qualified fourth and he was seventh or eighth in his Lotus 48 on Firestone tyres, which weren't really in the same class as our Dunlops that weekend.

Jimmy, Graham and I drove to the track together. They dropped me off first and that was the last I saw of Jimmy. He crashed in the first heat. But I do remember his mechanic driving the Lotus up and down the paddock all morning, trying to cure that misfire.

> There's just no doubt about it. That's how Jimmy died.

I'm absolutely certain in my own mind that misfire was the reason behind his death. I've always believed it, despite having read opinions and assessments of the accident from a host of other people, including Colin Chapman. We could go round that long right-hand curve where Jimmy crashed, side by side, even in the rain, at around 150 mph. But it wasn't a place where you wanted to deal with a problem.

I think Jimmy was having a terrible time with that misfire. Running alone, battling with a poor car on tyres which were not working terribly well, I reckon the engine suddenly cut out. He would have automatically applied a touch of opposite lock as the car began to slide – and then the power came back on, the rear end gripped, and the car suddenly speared off into the trees on the left of the track. In my mind, there's just no doubt about it. That's how Jimmy died.

It was an enormous tragedy which deeply affected all Jimmy's friends and rivals. I must say it got to me quite a bit. I know a lot of people died racing in those days and I'd experienced quite a bit of tragedy racing in Formula 3. The previous year I'd been in the Felday Brabham at Djurslandring in Denmark, when Peter Revson's brother Doug was killed and the race had been stopped. If you were really hardened to it you shrugged it off, or so I thought. But not at my age.

I honestly began wondering whether I was meant to be a racing driver at around this time. I mean, I just didn't have this ability to shrug it off. Now, of course, I know that none of the drivers has the ability to shrug it off. They just keep their feelings private, their worries to themselves.

I was reminded of this quite recently, a year or so ago, by Bob Wollek. Now you would have thought Bob was an undramatic, seasoned old campaigner who you might expect to be fairly philosophical about the risks involved. I think it may have been at Le Mans in 1986, just after poor Jo Gartner was killed during the night, when Bob said to me, 'I sometimes wonder why we do this. Is it worth dying for?'.

It really shook me. You see, it's not really the sort of thing you are used to discussing at the track. If I was with somebody I knew extremely well, perhaps, like David Hobbs, and we were away from the circuit having a quiet coffee together, it might be something we would touch on. But not at a track.

Bob's remarks also set me thinking a bit. I began to wonder: we're all getting a bit older and a bit wiser, hopefully, so why are we doing it? Sure as hell it's not for the money because, outside Formula 1, it's not that fantastic. We're basically doing it because we love it. Love the business of driving racing cars. Love the competition, the feeling of being involved.

At the other end of the scale, I have to say I will always remember Jacky Ickx mumbling, 'I don't know why I keep racing, maybe I should stop . . .' when we were sharing an Alfa Romeo at Mugello in 1975. Then, about ten seconds later, his face lit up. 'I know why we do it,' he smiled. 'Where else can we earn so much for doing so little!'

But Jimmy Clark's accident affected me for many years. I had used him as my yardstick. He'd done everything, won everything— Formula 1, Indianapolis, saloon cars, Formula 2—yet had never so much as broken his skin in a racing car accident. Consequently, when my wife and family said, 'Surely motor racing is dangerous,' I would point to Jimmy as an example of somebody who got away with it. A driver simply *has* to believe he is going to get away with it. So when it happened to Jimmy, it smashed my beliefs and philosophy.

'I know why we do it,' he smiled. 'Where else can we earn so much for doing so little!'

That spring and early summer of 1968 was tremendously busy and exciting for me, although it was not without its major problems and dramas. I didn't finish at Hockenheim after retiring in the second heat, but I was third behind Jochen Rindt and Piers Courage at the Easter Monday Thruxton international. I felt things were going well and was pretty optimistic about the future.

Also, around this time, I was offered a sports car drive at the Nurburgring in a Chevron B8 owned by Yorkshireman Tom Clapham. I turned up to test it, as arranged, at Silverstone, but the car was late arriving so I wandered up on to the pit balcony and watched as the Lotus team tried out its turbine cars in preparation for the Indy 500.

After a while, Colin Chapman looked up and said, 'Hello, you've been going pretty well this year, haven't you?' So I thought, wow, Colin Chapman spoke to me. 'Well, thank you very much,' I replied. He got on with whatever he was doing and some while later looked up again and said, 'How do you fancy trying one of these?' pointing to a completely new Lotus turbine car which had just been finished.

To say I accepted instantaneously would be a bit of an understatement! Chapman then asked me, 'Have you ever driven an automatic?' and I replied well, er, no, I hadn't, but he didn't bat an eyelid. 'Well, my Jaguar is out the back, so you'd better go and have a try,' he replied. So I nipped down from the balcony, tore up and down the central runway in his Jag a couple of times and then rushed back to the pits. 'Right, I know how to drive an automatic now,' I told him.

So there I am, sitting in the cockpit of this Lotus turbine car, helmet and overalls on, warming it up. They tell me that I'll have to wait until Graham Hill comes in with the second car because they are so quiet it's virtually impossible to hear where they are on the circuit. Apart from the whoosh of the turbine and the screech of the brake pads touching the discs, it was pretty well silent. So just as I'm waiting for my first run, Colin comes up and says, 'Derek, I'm sorry, but Graham's car has stopped out on the circuit, so he'll need to take over this one'. I got out and that was the end of the story. I never drove a Lotus again, and poor old Mike Spence was killed in one of those very cars qualifying for the Indy 500 a few weeks later.

Anyway, I did eventually get to the Nurburgring ready to drive Tom Clapham's Chevron, sharing with Geoff Breakell. I was really looking forward to this in a big way, because I'd always reckoned that the 'Ring was the most tremendous circuit in the world. With over 150 corners to each 14-mile lap, it was always a sensational challenge and I grew to love the place like no other track in the world. Anyway, here at last was my first chance to race on it.

Unfortunately, Tom's Chevron arrived late. We missed Friday practice. Then it hadn't turned up on Saturday morning and we missed the first session on that day. So, by the time it finally arrived in the paddock and we were all ready to go there was about an hour and a half left for us both to learn the circuit and qualify for the race.

Tom reckoned that Geoff should drive it first, so off he went. After starting his first flying lap, he never appeared again! About an hour later, news came back that the Chevron was parked down at Adenau bridge—totally undamaged, but stranded with ignition trouble.

That was the last we heard of it for another hour and a half. Then a truck arrived in the paddock. It was carrying the Chevron – or rather, the remains of the Chevron. It had been completely wrecked! I just couldn't figure out what on earth was happening!

Old Geoff was absolutely ashen-faced about the whole affair. So Tom said to him, 'I thought you stopped with electrical problems'. Breakell said, 'Aye, that's right Tom. But then this guy popped his head over the hedge and asked me if he could give me a tow back to the paddock. So I said, Ta very much, that's a good idea'.

So the pair of them rolled the car out on to the road, hitched it up behind this guy's Mercedes and started off towing it down the road back to the paddock, parallel with the main straight.

It turned out that the Mercedes bloke began to go faster and faster, with Geoff hanging on for dear life in the cockpit of the Chevron. Unfortunately Geoff had loosened the rear engine cover

A taste of F2 success! On the rostrum (right) at Nurburgring after finishing third in the 1968 Eifelrennen in the BT23C. Winner Chris Irwin is in the centre, flanked by second-place finisher Kurt Ahrens on the left.

when he'd stopped on the circuit, hoping he might be able to fix the problem with a poke about in the engine bay.

Suddenly, there was this bloody great crash as the wind got under the engine cover and lifted it up vertically behind the car. Breakell had immediately looked over his shoulder and, at precisely the same moment, matey in the Mercedes had slammed on his brakes. So the Chevron went smashing into the back of our helpful friend's car and that was the end of that. It was also the end of my first outing in a sports car!

A few weeks later I went back to the Nurburgring to finish third in the Eifelrennen with my own Brabham. The race was won by Chris Irwin's Lola ahead of Kurt Ahrens, also in a Brabham. It was held on the challenging little South Circuit which was so bumpy and spectacular you just wouldn't believe it. But it was another promising result for me, strengthening my feeling that I was really beginning to get the hang of this Formula 2 business.

Following this race I was absolutely amazed to receive a phone call from Keith Ballisat, Shell's representative at the races, saying that Ferrari were interested in talking to me. They were running their own Formula 2 programme at the time with the neat little Dino 166s, and the original idea was that I should test the car brought over for Jacky Ickx to drive at the Whit Monday Crystal Palace international. But Jacky shunted it, just as I shunted my Brabham, so it was organized that I should go down to Monza to try the car.

A touch of opposite lock at Crystal Palace during the Whit Monday international in '68, my Brabham just ahead of Jack Oliver's Lotus 48. On this occasion I crashed . . .

Everything was getting extremely hectic. Just to complicate matters I had received an approach from Major Owens, who ran the business side of the Cooper Grand Prix team, asking me whether I wanted to consider driving for them. Cooper, of course, had been one of the pioneers of the rear-engined Grand Prix car concept, though by 1968 were very much also-rans. But first of all I had to go down to Maranello to see Mr Ferrari himself.

I flew to Milan and drove down to Modena, stayed the night and then drove out to Maranello the next morning. Almost inevitably, it was one of Italy's national holidays as I recall. I was being shown round the factory by this little chap who was one of Ferrari's secretaries – he didn't like having women working in the factory in those days. We were in the race shop when I saw this tall, distinguished and very elegant-looking white-haired man walking down towards us between the rows of racing cars. He had dark tinted glasses and a white raincoat draped over his shoulders.

'Here comes the Commendatore, he's the one on the left.'

Walking beside him is a very short bloke, little more than five feet tall. 'Here comes the Commendatore,' said my secretary friend, 'he's the one on the left'. He must have thought I was dumb enough not to know. We lunched at the Cavallino restaurant, just over the road from the Ferrari factory gates. Ferrari talked endlessly about how wonderful Jochen Rindt was and then I flew home.

The next day I was up at Silverstone testing one of the old 1967 Cooper-Maseratis. By that time the team was using the new BRM V12 engines in its cars, but this was a testing hack left over from the previous year. I was not very impressed. Fair enough, I was young and pretty inexperienced, but it felt a ponderous old truck to me. I wondered, well, perhaps that's how all Formula 1 cars feel. But, deep down inside, I knew it wasn't really much good and I was not terribly interested.

I dropped by the Cooper factory to talk terms with John Cooper. But I put off making any serious commitment until I had completed a Ferrari test at Monza. I was invited down to try one of the Dino 166s with a view to driving it in the Monza Lottery Formula 2 Grand Prix. That was a very important race in Italy, so I was obviously excited by the prospect.

Contrary to what Tony Lanfranchi said in his book, it was not a case of those who could afford to pay the air fare going and other invited drivers staying at home. Ferrari picked up the tabs for the expenses. Anyway, I arrived at Monza where I found that several Italian drivers—Mario Casoni, Tino Brambilla and a bunch of others—were also going to have a try.

Twice I raced Ferrari's F2 Dino 166 in the Monza Lottery. In '68 it was on my maiden outing for Ferrari, when I qualified on pole only to become embroiled in a multiple shunt during the race. A year later I finished fifth on my last single-seater outing for Maranello . . .

I was quicker than any of them, which was obviously very pleasing. Immediately afterwards I drove straight down to Modena, checked into a hotel and motored out to Maranello the next morning. As I recall, it was another of those Italian national holidays, but there were still plenty of people working in the racing department. The race shop was absolutely immaculate. Seeing those superb racing cars on their shoulder-high trestles on that splendidly polished tiled floor made a big impression on me. Perhaps it wouldn't be regarded as a big deal by the lavish standards of today's top Grand Prix teams, but at the time it seemed to me like the last word in high technology.

There was a Can-Am car, a hill-climb car, three Formula 1s and two Formula 2s. The mechanics bustled round the place getting me step ladders to climb up into the cockpit. One guy asked me how I wanted the pedals positioned, another what shape gear lever knob I required and a third how much padding I wanted in the cockpit. He was carrying this folder containing a cross-sectional drawing of the car. When I told him where I wanted him to position the padding, he just drew it in on the diagram at the appropriate place.

They wanted me to sign immediately, but I was still hedging. To be honest, I'd heard so many stories about Ferrari and the way in which they had wrecked the careers of some drivers that I was still a little apprehensive. I wouldn't exactly say that I'd been in protected surroundings with our little Church Farm operation, but I knew precisely where I stood with my own car. Now, all of a sudden, I was facing the big-time world of hard-nosed professional motor racing. I asked if I could leave off signing my contract until after the Monza Lottery race.

When I got back to England I spoke to Coopers again. They made it clear that they wanted to sign me for Formula 1. This is it, I thought. The big break. The thought of a huge retainer danced through my mind. I mean, it had to be £10,000 at least, didn't it?

I went back to see Major Owens. When we got on to the subject of money he said, 'Well, we haven't had many decent results recently. Times are hard'. Oh well, I thought, perhaps I'll only get £5,000. He continued. 'We have lost our fuel sponsor and it's really a struggle to keep going.' I began to think I would have to muddle by on £2,500. Then he added, 'Of course, our starting money is based on the Mayfair Agreement and we didn't perform too well last season'. The Mayfair Agreement governed the financial side of Grand Prix racing at the time and starting money was based on performances the previous year. A bit like the Concorde Agreement in Grand Prix racing today, I would imagine.

'How about a purely nominal figure as a retainer for three years?' he suggested. 'Say five pounds...'

In the end, Major Owens got round to making me an offer. 'How about a purely nominal figure as a retainer for three years?' he suggested. I wanted to see what he was going to suggest. 'Say five pounds . . .'

This was one of the genuinely few occasions in my life that I was rendered utterly speechless. I think I muttered something about it being 'rather unrealistic', but he had another strong card in his hand which he immediately played.

He asked me, point blank: 'What the hell do you want out of your racing? When you first started, what were you aiming for?' Well, I told him, Formula 1. 'Here you are then,' said the Major triumphantly, 'we're offering you a drive and you are turning it down'. I told them I was prepared to do a deal until the end of the 1968 season, but Major Owens was too wise for that. He pointed out to me that, if I performed well, another team might come in with a big offer and snap me up for the following year. Coopers would not do a deal on that basis. In the end, they got Robin Widdows.

Down at Monza, I qualified on pole for the Lottery. Compared with the Cosworth FVA in my Brabham, the Dino 166 had no power except right at the top end. That's how I qualified fastest. Of course, in the race when you were slipstreaming hard with 16 other guys you could never break away and use that top-end advantage. It was a jewel of a chassis, but not much fun to drive in Formula 2 trim.

I was in amongst the leading bunch when the car suddenly swapped ends coming out of the Parabolica. My spin triggered off the most horrendous shunt, which saw three of the works Dinos wiped out of the race and Jean-Pierre Jaussaud hurled from his Tecno. He broke both legs, but was probably very lucky to be thrown out because the car caught fire. Thankfully, he made a full recovery and went on to race against me regularly.

God, why on earth hadn't I signed that contract before the race? What was I thinking about? Naturally, I figured that was the end of any chances I had with Ferrari, but it wasn't the case. When I returned to England there was a telegram waiting for me. It was an invitation to go to Modena and test a Grand Prix Ferrari. The big time at last!

However, life in the Bell family was pretty complicated and tense at the time. My wife Pam was terribly ill with what turned out to be colitis, aggravated by the birth of our son Justin and hardly helped by her anxiety about my racing. She went into hospital at around this time and there were a few days during which we were all desperately concerned about her. At one point we actually feared she might die. So when I returned from the Monza Lottery to find that telegram waiting for me, I was in a bit of a dilemma.

One thing was certain. My mother was implacably opposed to me going back to Italy. I remember walking into her house and she stood there and told me that I would never be allowed back in the house again if I went down to Modena for that test drive. So I went to see Pam in hospital and, very tactfully, edged round to the subject. She was amazed that I even had any doubts. 'Of course you must go,' she said firmly, 'it's just a chance you can't afford to pass up'. I was always very grateful to Pam for her understanding.

Off I went back to Italy for my first drive in a Formula 1 Ferrari. It was wet and gloomy when I reached the old autodrome, but Ferrari's chief engineer Mauro Forghieri was on hand to keep an eye on me. Just to keep my sense of proportion he lent into the cockpit and said,

Nerve-racking moment. My first run in a Ferrari Grand Prix car at Modena, late Spring 1968, watched by a concerned Mauro Forghieri. He warned me, 'Derek, if you crash today, you will never drive a red car again . . .'

On the grid, in the cockpit and on the circuit. My début at the wheel of a Grand Prix Ferrari in the 1968 Oulton Park Gold Cup. I ran steadily in the middle of the field, but retired with gearbox trouble. It was a glorious moment.

very quietly, 'Derek, I want you to know that if you damage this car at all, you will never drive a red car again. A green one, perhaps, but never a red one'. I got the impression he was only half-joking . . .

Despite the fact that there were puddles down at the tricky Esses section, I got down to within a couple of seconds of the outright lap record. To me, the car felt absolutely tremendous. I obviously had a great deal to learn about Formula 1, but Forghieri was very clued-up about the business of dealing with new drivers and he had plenty of sensible advice to offer. He kept reminding me that it was my first time out, that F1 cars have hidden vices and when they do snap out of control they break away so fast that you don't know what has happened until you have finished spinning.

'Derek, I want you to know that if you damage this car at all, you will never drive a red car again.'

I had been put down as a possible reserve entry for the Gold Cup meeting at Oulton Park in August, but they were obviously pretty impressed with my performance at Modena because I was asked to prepare a telegram in English asking the race organizers if they would accept a third entry. They also strongly hinted that I might have a run at Monza in the Italian Grand Prix if I did well on my home ground.

Chris Amon and Jacky Ickx were the regular Ferrari drivers in the team at the same race. I didn't do too badly, qualifying eighth and running just behind Pedro Rodriguez's BRM and ahead of Jochen Rindt's Brabham. I couldn't get past Pedro. I mean, I was so naïve that I didn't like to try taking the liberty, and, anyway, he never once looked in his mirrors. Eventually I retired with gearbox problems.

I then went to Monza for the Italian Grand Prix, where I qualified seventh and was holding seventh place when a piston blew. I parked out on the circuit and was walking back to the pits when I saw my team-mate Chris Amon go flying over the barriers into the trees at one of the fast Lesmo corners. He had lost control on oil dropped by John Surtees's Honda and I was absolutely certain that he must have been killed.

Coming only a few months after Jimmy's death, this seemed like the last straw. I trudged back to the pits thinking to myself, well, you can pack up and retire now and at least know that you drove a Formula 1 Ferrari in the Italian Grand Prix at Monza. When I got back to the pits, I learned that Chris had survived unscathed, so those thoughts subsided from my mind.

Monza was something else in that Ferrari! Apart from the fact that it was *very* fast in those days before they slowed it all down with

On the grid at Monza prior to my first Grand Prix start in the Ferrari. Running just outside the top six, it blew a piston and I retired – just in time to watch team-mate Amon go over the barrier into the trees . . .

chicanes everywhere, the Ferraris were fitted with rear wings that were activated by pressure on the brake pedal. If you went hard on to the brakes then the wing flipped up, as it also did if you went down as low as third gear. In addition, it had a manual over-ride as well. You needed that because the Curva Grande, for example, was all but flat-out, but a very tricky corner for all that. If you got carried away in a dice and then forgot to flick the switch going into a fast corner, you really were into heaps of trouble!

After Jacky Ickx broke his leg during the Canadian Grand Prix at Mosport Park I was also invited to drive in the US Grand Prix at Watkins Glen, but that was a pretty inconsequential affair and I retired with engine failure. I ended the year not really knowing what the future held as far as my Grand Prix career was concerned. I had only signed to drive Ferrari's Formula 2 cars, so everything was left rather up in the air.

The next thing on the agenda turned out to be a trip to Australia and New Zealand to do the Tasman Series over the winter of '68/'69. Amon had got together a deal to run a couple of Formula 2 166s fitted with 2.4-litre V6 engines. It was quite a relaxed affair in many way, with Ferrari just providing the cars and Chris getting the rest of it organized. From the factory's point of view, it was very low-key.

Ray Wardell, our mechanic at Church Farm Racing, went out to Maranello with our Ford Transit to collect the cars on a double up-and-over trailer loaned from David Piper. I flew down and drove back with him. These days you would send a £150,000 transporter on

Above *Underpowered in its four-cylinder Dino 166 form, once equipped with the 2.4-litre V6 'Tasman' engine the 1968 F2 Ferrari was a well-balanced jewel of a car, a real joy to drive.*

Right *Ray Wardell, for so long my mechanic at Church Farm Racing, casts an eye over the cockpit of my Ferrari Dino 166 at Tulln-Langenlebarn, July 1968.*

such a trip, but not in 1968. I met up with Ray at Aosta where we had a major drama at the customs.

Can you imagine the scene? Two confused Englishmen with a Transit van and a trailer carrying two single-seater Ferraris, en route to England to go to Australia and New Zealand! The Italian customs officials were totally confused. I'm not sure they thought that it was a dodgy business, but they did look pretty doubtful themselves. So they made us wait.

I remember we had to stay all day at the customs post because there was a football game on and these damn officials kept rushing off to hear how their team was doing. Ray was delayed there from four in the morning until four the following afternoon. Once the officials had finished their lunch and the football match was over, one of them just came sauntering out, signed our papers and we were free to go.

You would have thought that an organization like Ferrari would have provided all the necessary paperwork, but no. We didn't have the right documents and just had to sit it out until they decided to let us through. From then on it was no problem.

That whole Tasman trip was really fantastic. The team was run by Chris's personal mechanic Roger Bailey—who now runs the ARS series in North America.

I finished fourth in the New Zealand Grand Prix, but then blew up my engine in the final of the race at Levin after leading Jochen Rindt's works Lotus 49T in one heat. We only had one spare engine for my car, so that was all I had left for the rest of the series—five more races. Chris still had a spare one for his car, of course, but because he was team leader he kept that, and rightly so. So we agreed that I

On the grid at Vallelunga with Roger Bailey, Chris Amon's personal mechanic at Ferrari and the man who looked after our Dino 246s in the following winter's Tasman series. Roger is now in charge of the ARS racing series in the United States.

would drive with fewer revs for the rest of the series, but I still managed second to Chris in the Australian Grand Prix at Lakeside and second to Jochen in the wet at Warwick Farm.

It was a great series to compete in, particularly for me at that stage of my career. There I was, lined up against the best in the world and I certainly learned a great deal. Chris never won a World Championship, nor even a Grand Prix, but he was tremendously talented and always ran at the front. I had great respect for him. Jochen Rindt wasn't too shabby either.

With seven races in six weeks, split between New Zealand and Australia, the schedule was pretty hectic to say the least. In a group with Jochen, Graham, Chris, Frank Gardner and Piers Courage there were obviously going to be a lot of laughs. But there were also some serious moments, one of which has stuck very vividly in my mind. I've referred back to it on many occasions since.

It concerned an incident on the grid at Teretonga, the final round of the New Zealand leg of the series, before we went over to Australia. I was on the second row of the grid behind Chris and Jochen, while Graham was right behind me on row three. I was still really a raving young Formula 2 driver and, when the flag dropped, I just let the clutch in with a bang. Jochen appeared to move at the same moment, but the Lotus only lurched forward a few feet. It had broken a drive shaft!

Of course, I just slammed into the back of him. Boom! He shot forward again, so I dipped the clutch thinking that he was really starting this time. Boom! I hit him again, vaulted over one of his rear wheels and was away. That Dino 246 was certainly a tough little car; you wouldn't want to pull a stunt like that in most of today's single-seaters. Despite the fact that the impact had deranged the steering, I still managed to finish fifth.

Graham just fixed me with a stare. 'It's not funny,' he said firmly, 'it's just stupid.'

After the race, Jochen didn't say a word. It was Graham who raised the subject. We were sitting at a party that same evening and he said casually, 'What the hell were you up to today?'. So I tried to make a joke of it and replied, 'Oh, I was trying to get rid of your team-mate,' knowing full well that there was some aggro between him and Jochen.

Graham just fixed me with a stare. 'It's not funny,' he said firmly, 'it's just stupid. If I'd let my clutch out as well there would have been the most monumental accident. You don't just go when the flag comes down, you go when the bloke in front of you goes.'

After a moment's reflection, it all seemed very obvious. I always remembered that comment and have reminded various young drivers, including my son Justin, that it is a point worth thinking about. You can't win the race on the starting grid, but you certainly can lose it with manoeuvres like that!

That trip came to an end all too soon and I had to face the task of sorting out what was going to happen in 1969. I knew Ferrari couldn't really guarantee me anything. As it turned out I drove just one more Formula 1 race for them, the International Trophy at Silverstone. We just floundered around in the rain on our unsuitable Firestones and I trailed home ninth. Chris was tenth.

It was a difficult time for Ferrari. They had big financial problems and were on the verge of being taken into the Fiat empire, so I never knew quite where I stood. I was always hoping and praying that I would get another Formula 1 chance, because I knew that the flat-12 boxer engine was in the pipeline. We did some more Formula 2 races, but the Dinos could not now keep pace with the 1968 series Cosworth FVA engines run by the opposition, so it was a fiasco.

At the Monza Lottery, for example, we didn't have the sort of performance advantage we had enjoyed the previous summer, although I did manage to finish fifth which I suppose was better than getting involved in a bloody great shunt. Overall, though, what Clay Regazzoni and I found difficult to believe was that these were the cars which had been taken out to the Argentine for the Temporada the previous winter and won just about everything in sight. With the greatest respect, I don't think Brambilla and de Adamich were that brilliant compared with Clay and myself, so I always believed there had to be something, let's say *unusual*, about those cars they ran in South America.

The Monza Lottery marked the end of Ferrari's Formula 2 programme, so I found myself at a loose end again, but I did get the chance to drive the four-wheel-drive McLaren M9A in the British Grand Prix at Silverstone.

I never even tested the car prior to the race because it was a real last-minute affair. Bruce McLaren had driven it in the rain at Goodwood on the Wednesday before making the decision to enter the car for the Grand Prix, so I was phoned up the day before first practice. As I understood it, the idea was to run with only very small wings, but both Bruce and Denny Hulme decided that they wanted small wings on their conventional, two-wheel-drive M7s. Unfortunately the team didn't have three sets of small wings available, so the M9A was fitted with a bloody great shovel affair at the back, rather like the one used on the Formula 5000 car which we were running out of Church Farm for Peter Gethin.

It was a right royal handful. Its handling characteristics were completely different to a conventional car. Instead of the front wheels tucking into the apex of a corner when you backed off the throttle, the M9A just wanted to lurch straight on. I found that the only way to get it through the corner was to back off the throttle momentarily,

give a great wrench on the steering wheel and then go hard on to the power again.

Under braking it was pretty frightening too. You had to have the brake balance tailored to match the power split between the front and the rear wheels. I don't think that was ever successfully achieved because it had a mind of its own, so I quickly learned to keep about two feet away from the edge of the circuit when I went on the brakes because I felt it would just disappear off the track and wanted to leave myself a bit of a margin.

I qualified right at the back, with all the other four-wheel-drive cars and it broke its rear suspension a few laps into the race. Afterwards, sitting in the caravan talking it over, Bruce turned to me and said, 'What do you reckon, Derek? Will it make it or won't it?' I said that I didn't think it would and that was it. It was never seen again. Nor me, almost!

I had been through such a diabolical season in Europe that I needed something to restore my reputation.

By this stage I was getting a bit desperate. Earlier in the year we'd met up with Tom Wheatcroft who was obviously a great enthusiast and he'd said, 'Lad, if I can ever be of any assistance, I'd love to help you'. I never thought about it very much at the time, but the Ferrari deal turned out to be such a disaster that I began to think in terms of doing the Tasman series again towards the end of the summer.

I had been through such a diabolical season in Europe that I needed something to restore my reputation. So, when the chance came up to buy an ex-works Brabham BT26A, we got in touch with Tom and did a deal. There were only a couple of Cosworth DFW 2.5-litre Tasman engines in existence and we bought them from Lotus. To be honest, they were not in the best condition when we got our hands on them.

One of the biggest problems with the Brabham was its tyres. Tom had a close relationship with Dunlop, so we used their rubber although the car had been designed to work on Goodyears. It was awful! I just couldn't make it work. I finished second in the New Zealand Grand Prix, but it was a real handful and I started feeling very depressed.

Thankfully help was at hand, or so it seemed. Chris Amon had been spectating and saw how nervous and twitchy the car was out on the circuit. He said, 'Come on Derek, I'll take it out and give it a run. I'll sort it out for you'. So Chris had a try in it at Levin – and blew up the engine after about 12 laps. It was just one of those things, not his fault at all. But that was one engine out of the bloody window and I was back in the same position as I'd been the year before with only one engine left.

Opposite *At about the time my Ferrari contract was dying under me, I was released to drive the four-wheel-drive M9A in its sole race outing, the 1969 British Grand Prix at Silverstone. It was something of a spooky experience, to say the least, and didn't last for long!*

Above *Great little car! The Wheatcroft Racing Brabham BT30 which we ran out of Church Farm in our 1970 European F2 Trophy onslaught. It was a season which revived my self-confidence and produced some tremendous results.*

Right *Top form! I felt super-confident before the F2 race at Barcelona in 1970, where I drove one of the best races of my life. Here I'm leading Henri Pescarolo's similar BT30 off the line at Montjuich Park while, behind me, the Tecnos of François Cevert and Clay Regazzoni have boxed in Ronnie Peterson's March 702.*

You've guessed it! The remaining engine blew up in the Lady Wigram Trophy race at Christchurch, so we just packed up and came home. When we arrived back in England we got hold of a set of used Goodyears from Brabham, slapped them on the car and I went round Goodwood a second and a half quicker than my best Dunlop time. Not that it mattered, of course, because my career seemed to be falling apart. Everything I did turned to ullage. It was awful.

Tom Wheatcroft came to my rescue again. I phoned him up and said, look, I haven't got anything. How about running an F2 car? We'll order a Brabham BT30 and run it from Church Farm with my old friend Mick Earle. It was absolutely the right thing to do, in my opinion.

It was a fantastic, absolutely classic season. After all that disappointment with Ferrari we were right back in the swim of things, running at a million miles an hour. It did wonders for my confidence. Third at Thruxton behind Stewart and Rindt, fourth at Pau, third at Hockenheim and then a win at Barcelona after one of the best drives of my life.

Of course, we still had the BT26 and were tempted into taking it to the Belgian Grand Prix at Spa, just to test the temperature of the

water in F1. Before we could do that we had to change the aluminium fuel tanks because the regulations now required rubber bag tanks, so we had to have those specially made up. But we were totally out of our depth. I still wasn't really very experienced in setting up a chassis. I mean, I knew about roll bars and shock absorbers, but not much else.

It was another catastrophe! I figured if I could just get into the race, I might have a chance of getting my act sorted out. Of course, the gear lever had to break on the warming-up lap and I came round to the grid stuck in third. End of story. If I hadn't had the Formula 2 programme up and running, I reckon I would have stuck my head in an oven . . .

Financially, though, it was a hard time. Everybody has always thought I was very nicely fixed, even then, but the only income I had regularly in 1970 was as farm manager. That was £20 a week. Justin was 18 months old and my daughter Melanie only three months old, so it seemed to be one hell of a small amount to keep a family on, run a road car and all the rest of it. At the end of the year I wound up runner-up in the European Formula 2 Championship behind Clay Regazzoni in the Tecno.

At the end of the season John Surtees offered me a drive in the United States Grand Prix at the Glen in his latest TS7, but he wanted the use of an engine as part of the deal. We loaned him the fated engine out of the Brabham and the car ran well.

I had just managed to overtake Reine Wisell's Lotus 72 for about sixth or seventh place when the clutch suddenly began to vibrate like hell. I just couldn't stand the thought of another retirement, so I

Above *A second or so after taking the chequered flag to win the Barcelona race ahead of Emerson Fittipaldi's Lotus 69 which is just approaching the man with the chequered flag in this shot. Like Le Mans eleven years later, this was one race I felt was mine from the outset!*

Right *Four wheels off the deck at Nurburgring during the non-title F2 race held the same day as the German Grand Prix took place further down the autobahn at Hockenheim. I never managed to win a single-seater race at the 'Ring, retiring on this occasion and being overtaken on the last lap by Jochen Mass's March two years later.*

*I felt I had struck up a good working relationship with John Surtees, seen (**right**) discussing the Surtees TS7 with me in the pits at Watkins Glen where I drove it in the 1970 United States Grand Prix. **Below** Out on the circuit chasing Reine Wisell's Lotus 72 which eventually finished third. I wound up sixth, watching the revs.*

eased back a thousand revs or so and drove to finish. Wisell wound up third. I was sixth, scoring the only World Championship point of my Formula 1 career.

Tom Wheatcroft had been a terrific supporter. I always felt he was tremendously interested in my progress and, by the end of 1970, I think it was in the back of old Surtees's mind that he might pay for me to do F1 the following year. In fact Tom and I went to talk it over with John and, basically, if we could have found some more sponsorship then I think it might well have come off.

However, I was a bit naïve about these things. I went off to Kyalami for the sports car race and by the time I'd returned, Rolf Stommelen had nipped in and secured the drive. With £30,000 sponsorship! It seemed like a pretty big deal at the time.

In fairness, John offered me a Formula 5000 programme, but in my own mind I'd always rather seen that as a backwater for people who had never really made it. I declined the offer, but he still ran me in a third car in the British Grand Prix at Silverstone the following summer. In retrospect, it might not have been a bad idea to have accepted that F5000 deal. In the end, Mike Hailwood drove the Formula 5000 Surtees and had quite a good season with it.

At the start of 1971 I still did not have any Formula 1 racing arranged, although Tom Wheatcroft dusted down his old March 701 and I drove it in two non-championship races at the start of the season. In the Buenos Aires Grand Prix I was running third when our dear old engine broke a camshaft, and I finished way down in 15th

Leading the opening lap of the 1971 Eifelrennen, ahead of François Cevert, Ronnie Peterson, the late Gerry Birell, my Williams March team-mate Henri Pescarolo and Carlos Reutemann. This time fading oil pressure ended my race.

place at the end of the Questor Grand Prix, that one-off race at Ontario Motor Speedway in California where Formula 1 and Formula 5000 were mixed in together.

The old March was prepared and entered by Frank Williams who had a similar car of his own which was being driven by Henri Pescarolo. I always had a lot of time for Frank and the single-minded way he went about his motor racing. I got the opportunity to drive in a few Formula 2 outings in one of his March 712s that season, and we had some quite promising races.

I led the Eifelrennen at Nurburgring, ahead of Ronnie Peterson, François Cevert and all the other so-called young lions, but the engine suddenly lost its oil pressure and I pulled off out on the circuit. And at Thruxton I really ought to have won, but I spun off trying to get past Graham and Ronnie into the chicane.

What a move! What a hero! I reckon it was one of the few times in my career I was just cruising along. I seemed to be all over them both and figured it was only a matter of time before I cracked them under braking for the chicane just before the pits. I decided that I would practice the manoeuvre and dropped back slightly so that I had a clear track in front of me.

Getting it wrong! Spinning to a halt on Jo Siffert's oil with the Frank Williams March 712M, Easter Monday Thuxton meeting, 1971. My mum saw it all from the grandstand . . .

However, what I didn't bank on was my Porsche team-mate Jo Siffert. His Chevron's engine blew up and good old Jo trailed into the pits pouring oil all over the track. I came flying up into the braking area and, that's right, round I went. My mother was there, sitting in the grandstand at the chicane, having decided at long last to come and

see a motor race for the first time. She shrieks out 'darling, darling . . .' and the Old Man's next to her muttering 'stupid bugger' . . . I felt a real prawn and wound up third, which is where I was running before I spun.

As I've mentioned, I drove a third Surtees entry in the British Grand Prix, but it didn't last long and I retired with broken rear suspension quite early in the race. In single-seater terms you could say that was the last vaguely competitive Formula 1 car I ever drove, although we'll return later to the matter of the Formula 1 Tecno and my stint with Team Surtees in 1974.

As Ferrari said in 1971, when somebody asked him why he didn't try me again, 'I never re-warm cold soup'.

I suppose, on reflection, once I had been to Ferrari and tasted Formula 1, in some ways I had reached the peak of my single-seater career. As Ferrari said in 1971, when somebody asked him why he didn't try me again, 'I never re-warm cold soup'.

That was a pretty crushing remark, really, but I suppose it was fair comment. It brought home to me the fact that I'd briefly touched the pinnacle of the sport and then tumbled down again. Second time round was much harder and people were not going to be so excited. In 1970 I reckon I was quite impressive running against Rindt, Peterson and Cevert, but it didn't have the same effect for my career. I'd been there before.

The new guys got the breaks. People thought, 'Bell's had his crack at Formula 1' and then went on to choose other promising newcomers. I knew that was the general feeling within the business, so I was thankful that my career began to develop along a distinctively different route.

Chapter 2

Personalities and problems

THAT'S an interesting title for a chapter! During my career I met plenty of both and I suppose you could say that the Colonel was top of both lists! I was born in 1941 and when I was nine years old we moved to Pagham, where I still live to this day. My mother was obviously in love with the Colonel who had three daughters from his first marriage so, what with me and my sister, there was a family of five to look after.

I'm always impressed with how well my mother dealt with bringing us all up together. I always got on very well with my father, who died in 1985, but my parents split up when I was very young and ultimately both went their own way and became happily married a second time. My father worked in BBC television and subsequently remarried a delightful New Zealand lady named Joy, with whom he was very happy.

I don't think my parents' divorce was particularly acrimonious, but it just took time for it to be finalized. So, basically, I spent all my time as a kid down here at Pagham and, as early as 1949, I think, I was able to crash round the farm learning to drive.

Of course, the Colonel wasn't the Colonel then. At the time I just knew him as Uncle Bernard. He became 'the Colonel' when I was driving with Peter Westbury at Felday Engineering. They had been involved in building a four-wheel-drive hill-climb car using Ferguson transmission and, of course, Major Tony Rolt was the boss of that company. He was called 'the Major', so old Jim Charman, a great character who was one of the Felday mechanics, said, 'Right, we're going to call you Colonel, do you know that?'. And the name stuck.

It was much easier for everybody to call him the Colonel rather than getting into that embarrassing situation where some people are calling him Bernard, others calling him Mr Hender and the rest not

A personality and a problem! My stepfather Bernard Hender – 'The Colonel' to all and sundry in motor racing – alongside the Formula 1 Tecno PA123 in the pits at Clermont-Ferrand during practice for the 1972 French Grand Prix. I owe the Colonel an enormous debt of gratitude for how he helped my professional racing career – rather more than I can say of the Tecno!

quite sure how to address him. Anyway, in those glorious 'Uncle Bernard' days driving became second nature to me. There were tractors and jeeps on the farm and I had a wonderful, really wonderful, childhood down there.

Some of my earliest memories of driving a tractor are of going out to mow the grass in our caravan site when I was about 12 or 13. I used to have one of these big rotary mowers on a big platform. Towing it around, reversing in and out of the caravans, I was a star. I spent hours doing this and, of course, there were plenty of girls on the site, which always held my attention. But at the same time I was earning pocket money doing this work, so I never had the sort of childhood that many kids have, bumming around aimlessly and causing general aggravation. I was out working all the time, as were my mother and the Colonel. They never stopped, it seemed to me.

It was terrific. I mean, what 12-year-old wouldn't love being out driving tractors all day? I've got a lot of happy memories of all that larking about. One incident I particularly recall involved this bloke called John Brown. He always looked like an American GI with his crew cut, khaki-coloured pants and boots and all that sort of thing. One day we were playing around and he threw a pitchfork which caught me right on the back of my leg. The bloody thing stuck there and I've still got the scar to this day!

I must have been 11 at the time, so we are talking about 35 years ago. I never heard of him again, until the autumn of 1987 when I got a letter from him which started 'You probably don't remember me . . .' So we got into contact and had a long chat on the phone. It was great to be reminded of those really happy times.

I was always content to stay on the farm during my holidays, preferring that to going up to my father in London. It wasn't that I didn't want to spend time with him, it was just that I loved life down at Pagham so much. I went to a local school, Rose Green, until I was 11, then to a prep school at Pangbourne and from there to King's School, Worcester. Finally I went to the Royal Agricultural College, but I always came back during my holidays. They were for the farm, first and foremost.

My relationship with the Colonel was not always easy while I was growing up. I got on with him all right, but he was quite an authoritarian, yet a very quiet man who didn't show his emotions very much. He can be quite abrupt with people who think a lot of him, not because he necessarily means to be, but that's just his way. Colonel was just the right title for him, believe me!

The staff here still go in fear and trepidation of him, even now. When they see him coming they're in there, shovelling away, thinking, 'God, we don't want the Old Man's wrath around our neck . . .' I know exactly how they feel. When I was working on the farm, he would *always* arrive on the scene when I was doing something I shouldn't be doing. If I was having a pee behind the wall, stopped to have a drink, got off the tractor to fix a plough shear, damn me, he would always turn up. Of course, he thought I'd been doing nothing else all day . . .

He could be a crusty old sod, no doubt about it, but he was a wonderful man and everybody has an enormous amount of affection for him. But one thing I must make clear – and this isn't intended to criticize him in any way – is that he was a different man at home to the one who used to come away with us to the races.

In 1959 I drove down to the Italian Grand Prix with him. I was only 17, but he trusted me to drive his Jaguar XK150. He would be dozing in the passenger seat as I edged it up from 100 mph to 110 mph, then to 115 mph, at which point one of his eyes would flicker open and he would growl, 'slow down!'. Thanks to him I had plenty of opportunities to drive high-performance sports cars at a young age. He loved nice cars and followed up the XK150 with an E-type, not only the first one in Sussex, but almost certainly the first one to be *crashed* in Sussex when he put it into a ditch!

Of course, what he didn't know is that I'd been poodling round the lanes with the XK150 back when I was only 15. While he was in the bar, I would thrash it up the road to Chichester and come back with it pretending that I'd just been for a whirl round the farmyard. But he was still rather a distant man who I found it hard to get really close to.

I suppose I really began to understand him when I was about 18 or 19. I had been working on the farm until nine o'clock at night and got a call from my mother asking me if I would go and pick some people up from Bognor Regis railway station. At that time I had a 1937 Morris, a really rowdy old truck which we'd bought for £40, so I quite naturally thought that I would take my mother's old Jaguar Mark Eight for the trip.

Anyway, after I had collected them, I took these people to a club just up the road from the farm and, to cut a long story short, eventually got back home about 11.30 at night. I strolled in to find mother and the Old Man waiting for me and they went absolutely ape. It was all 'what right do you think you have to take the big car?' and so on, and so on . . .

It stopped me absolutely in my tracks. I think I spluttered something about 'well, I never thought about it, to be honest . . . they were *your* friends.' It just cut me up like you wouldn't believe and I simply broke down in tears, there and then. I said to the Old Man, 'You never say thank-you for anything, never any gratitude for anything I do'. So he came over and put his hand on my shoulder. 'I'm incapable of saying it,' he explained softly, 'I'm just too shy to say it'.

It was difficult for me to understand at the time, but I think it helped me get to know his real character and qualities. His gruff demeanour really covers up his basic shyness as a man.

It sounds trite, but I have honestly never met anybody like him before. He did so much for me and, indeed, he still does a lot for me, and I like to think that I did something for him as well. I hope I brought him a lot of pleasure because he could share in my racing, my successes and my disappointments. If it hadn't been for coming away to the races with me, he would have just stayed on the farm. I got him away from all his boozy mates and introduced him to a circle of people he wouldn't otherwise have met.

He was 75 years old in November 1987, and is still terribly fit. He looks great, despite the fact that he never takes part in any outdoor sport. It's strange really, but he'll go to Spain with all his golfing mates and watch them play; he's President of the local cricket club and he'll be at every local match during the season. Yet·I've never known him play any game at all. It's odd, isn't it?

He never seemed to want to get embroiled with anything his own daughters were involved with, so I think my racing bridged a gap for him. In his early years he was too busy building up the farm to have any time or spare money for anything like that himself, so I was grateful for the very pragmatic approach he took to my racing back in 1966. He simply said, 'Look, Derek, it's obvious you want to go racing, so let's cut the farming out for the time being. You can always come back to it when you are 40, but you can't start motor racing at that age!'

For all his reticence, he was an amazingly passive man. When I used to bring that Lotus 41 back from abroad with wheels hanging off, he just forked out to have it repaired. There was never any tension or bad feeling at all. I couldn't have done it without him.

The Colonel's enthusiasm was quite remarkable. I mean, he would make a lot of trips abroad in my Formula 3 days to watch over my progress. There are endless stories about those early days, but my favourite involves going down to the 1966 Monaco F3 supporting event with the Lotus 41.

I drove down to Monaco in a Ford flat-deck truck which I'd bought from Roy Pike, the American driver who was one of F3's leading lights at the time and whose style at the wheel I tried hard to emulate. Geoff Evans, who was the best man at my wedding, and Mick Earle sat between the front and rear wheels of the Lotus, in the transporter, all the way from England to Monte Carlo. Ray Wardell and I were in the front. No, we didn't take turns and swap over – Ray and I drove all the way!

Geoff and Mick used to sleep in the transporter.

Ray and I stayed at the Hotel Westminster with the Colonel, who had flown down, while Geoff and Mick used to sleep in the transporter down in the car park. Once the Lotus had been unloaded, there was room for them to sleep with their heads underneath the lockers – which were about three feet deep – with their bodies stretching out into the open in sleeping bags down the back of the truck.

One night, we were returning from dinner and suddenly Geoff and Mick stopped in their tracks as they approached the pick-up truck. You wouldn't believe it, but a French couple were tucked up in the back, having it away. They were really brassed off by that, but tapped discreetly on the side of the Ford and asked 'would you mind if we come in?'

I failed to qualify for the race after a bit of a fiasco when Firestone came along and asked us if we would test a new type of cover for them. I suppose I thought well, being something new, they might have reasonable potential, but I should have realized it was a gamble when pacemakers such as Pike and Piers Courage decided they didn't want to use them. I just didn't have the experience to stand back for a few moments and think, 'Wait a minute, this is Monte Carlo. We've got half-an-hour of free practice and then 20 minutes of qualifying. And that's it'.

I should have opted for what we knew, but instead I took the attitude 'yeah, great . . . let's have a crack at that'. It was largely our fault that I didn't qualify. We should have said, 'no, thanks very much' to Firestone and perhaps tested them later, at Silverstone or somewhere. At any rate, I didn't make it into the race.

On the Saturday night we were storming round town, had a few drinks all over the place and ended up at the Tip Top bar.

The Tip Top is a long bar which is about ten feet wide at the point where it opens out on to the pavement. Geoff, Mick and I were sitting there eating something awful like curry and chips at three o'clock in the morning, and the Colonel, bless him, was up at the bar, looking a little the worse for wear.

Suddenly, we looked round and saw what were obviously two ladies of the night stepping down the bar on tiptoe and we looked at the floor to see it covered with water. At that point there was a shout from the bar as the guy standing next to the Colonel began shaping up to punch him. It appeared that the Old Man had fallen asleep at the bar, thought because he was standing up he was in a public loo and, consequently, peed all over the floor!

Can you imagine it? Peed all over the Tip Top bar! So this guy standing next to him leans over to put the old man's equipment away and, of course, got it all over his hands. Anyway, he got most upset and threatened to hit the Colonel, so we just ignored the whole affair and pretended it had nothing to do with us.

Eventually we poured the Old Man out of the place and immediately bumped into the father of John Hine, another of the English Formula 3 drivers. Anyway, he was also pretty merry, so in the end we managed to persuade them that they were not going to walk home and stuffed the two fathers into a taxi. The last we saw was them arguing about which way to go first, because John Hine's father was staying at Villefranche and we were all at Menton, like five miles in one direction and five miles in the other. Anyway, the Old Man got home safely, no doubt having won the day.

The following day we felt a bit frail, to say the least. Geoff, Mick and I were on the beach at about noon, definitely a bit on the secondhand side, and the Old Man still hadn't appeared. Then at about one o'clock he came striding down the beach as bold as brass. He *never* used to get a hangover!

'Morning Colonel!' 'Morning lads!' 'Well,' we said, 'did you let the side down last night, Colonel!' He replied, 'Why? What did I do? Hit a policeman, or something?' 'Oh no, a lot worse than that,' we said. 'Worse than that?' 'Yes,' we said, 'you peed all over the Tip Top bar!' 'Oh, is that all,' he said. And he was back in there the same evening, ordering cognac and sodas all round . . .

Of course, Mick Earle was another crucial personality who played a major part in my early career. I first met him in 1965 when I was doing my first season of single-seater racing in the old Lotus 31. He was living in Pagham with his first wife, Josie, and managed a local motor accessory shop called Hare Spares. I got to know him quite well in those early days, but after his marriage broke up he ended up living in Pagham on his own and I got to know him much better. We used to train together a lot at local gymnasiums, that sort of thing.

He was the sort of guy who had lots of ideas and was really good for Hare Spares, but his main aim was obviously to get mixed up with motor racing. In 1968 I started to get involved with him and, along with George Brown, who had previously worked for a local Jaguar dealership and strangely enough had built the engine for my Lotus Seven four years earlier, we all got my first Formula 2 programme on the road.

I think the Colonel paid Mick about five pounds a week, a real pittance, but none of us was earning any real money and we were all pretty hard pushed as I was trying to keep a family as well. But when you want to do something badly enough you just get on and do it, not really worrying too much about the money side of it all.

Braking for the Malmedy 'chicane' in the Wheatcroft Brabham BT26A during qualifying for the 1970 Belgian Grand Prix. The gear linkage fell apart on the warming-up lap!

So it was Mick and Ray Wardell who ran the BT23C in 1968, with George coming in later when Ray left us. Ray had been an apprentice at one of the local Hare garages, so that's how we got to know him. He came to us as a skinny, chain-smoking teenager; very enthusiastic and obviously extremely talented. The two of them continued to

work for Church Farm Racing after I went off to Ferrari in 1968, running the works McLaren Formula 5000 car for Peter Gethin with the Colonel the following year. Then in 1970, of course, I came back and Mick and George ran the orange Wheatcroft BT30, as by then Ray had gone off to join John Surtees.

Mick really came on tremendously during his years with us, but he would be the first to admit that he hated working with figures – apart from the feminine type. As far as accounts were concerned he was as bad as I was, something which was to lead us into trouble, as will be seen later.

But we had *such* a good time and enjoyed seemingly endless laughs. I like to think our team probably had more fun in motor racing in those Formula 2 days than just about anyone has done since. Formula 2 seemed to encourage that mood. Everybody involved in the business tended to stay in the same hotel and we all had dinner with the other teams and the journalists. We had a great time and, although we certainly raced hard, there was a tremendous feeling of camaraderie which I believe is severely lacking in racing these days.

Our team probably had more fun in motor racing in those Formula 2 days than just about anyone has done since.

After we finished in F2, Mick got involved with Rod Banting and put a deal together to run the Pygmee Formula 2 cars, but it all turned sour on them. That was probably the furthest I got from Mick, because he was struggling to make it on his own, and having a very tough time of it, while I was struggling to get my career back on the road. To be honest, the early 1970s were difficult times for us both.

Eventually Mick got it together and went to work for my close friend David Purley in Bognor, running first his Formula Atlantic and later his Formula 1 cars. Now, of course, he's become a very respected figure, his team, Onyx Racing, is absolutely meticulous and he's got the budget to do things properly. He's become a very wealthy lad through an enormous amount of hard effort helped, I may say, by his second wife Dinah who has been tremendously good for him. After those troubled days in the early 1970s I think she did a wonderful job in helping him to become motivated and organized in the right direction. I think that's fantastic.

Mick and I, of course, were at the sharp end of a major problem which arose with Tom Wheatcroft at the end of 1970, the season in which he had sponsored me in the orange Brabham BT30. I was at my motor accessory shop in Bognor one day when through the door came a writ. It was from Tom, suing me for all the money he had put into my racing programme the previous season. I just about dropped

Tom Wheatcroft squats by his March 701 as I prepare for the start of the 1971 non-championship Argentine Grand Prix at Buenos Aires. Tom was a crucial benefactor who helped me enormously in 1970.

dead on the spot. I couldn't believe it. I mean, a writ from Tom Wheatcroft. To say I was absolutely flabbergasted would not even make a start on it . . .

So I phoned him up and said, 'What are you doing to me? Why is this happening?' It was impossible. I just didn't have the £14,000, or whatever it was he was after. He just replied, 'Well, lad, that Mick Earle, 'e never got those accounts to me in time. So I figure that if I didn't get those accounts through in time to set against my tax, then I'll bloody well get it back another way!'

He was, in effect, trying to say that the backing he had given us was a loan, not sponsorship. Well, I just had to appeal to him. I said, 'Look Tom, I just *can't* pay you that sort of money. You *know* you sponsored me; you financed my year'. Yet there was nothing in writing between us. In those days I didn't believe that sort of thing was necessary with people you thought you knew well. I suppose that was a bit naïve, on reflection.

All right, I know Mick was utterly useless with accounts in those days – and he accepts that – but there was absolutely nothing irregular going on. We just hadn't got the figures together. I suppose it's a bit like somebody now asking for between £350,000 and £400,000 in 1988 terms; the cost of financing a season in Formula 3000.

Eventually the whole business was sorted out after letters had gone backwards and forwards from Tom to my solicitor and, in the end, he got the figures he wanted. It was agreed that the car, engines, spare wheels and equipment would be sold and he would get all the money from the sale.

It was a sad way for our partnership to finish because I had the feeling that, basically, I got on with him very well and we certainly had a lot of laughs together. It cast an interesting light on his personality; once he had made a decision to do something, there was no swaying him, even if it meant changing course in mid-stream. I remember hearing him talking about some deal on the phone to somebody. He'd suddenly say, 'That's it. I don't want to know. Finish!'. And that would be it.

Happily, it's all water under the bridge, a very long time ago. I get on fine with Tom now and always make a point of going across to chat with him and he always asks about my mother, my in-laws, how's the Colonel, that sort of thing. But there was certainly plenty of hard feeling at the time and, even today, looking back on the whole business absolutely staggers me!

By the end of that 1970 season I was getting a bit concerned how my career was going to develop, because I obviously still considered my future to lie with single-seaters. I still regarded myself as a single-seater man, but the offers were hardly flooding in. So for 1971 I made a move which, on reflection, must have been one of the most significant of my whole career. I joined the JW/Gulf team to drive in endurance events at the wheel of a factory Porsche 917, sharing with Jo Siffert.

This deal brought me into close contact with John Wyer, another very strong influence in my racing life. To be honest, he was a real disciplinarian, not so much from what he said to you, the driver, but simply from his overall attitude. You did what he asked and respected him a great deal. It was very much like being at school with John Wyer as the headmaster.

The first contact I had with the JW Gulf team was back in 1968 when I was driving for Ferrari. Le Mans had been delayed until September largely because of the French university riots that had taken place during the summer, and he contacted me to see whether I would be interested in driving one of his Ford GT40s.

At this point Ferrari did not want me to go to Le Mans, feeling I was insufficiently experienced. I'd never done the race before and, in fact, never raced a sports car of any sort. I went down to Thruxton with Wyer and tested a brand-new GT40. It didn't even have its side windows in, but I must have impressed him sufficiently because he asked me to share it with Pedro Rodriguez at Le Mans.

Of course, Ferrari would not release me to drive a Ford and the following week I received a telegram saying that they wanted me to drive in the United States Grand Prix. So I went out and did that, but at the same time had a long talk with David Yorke, who had really been the intermediary between me and the JW Gulf team.

'David,' I asked, 'what the hell am I going to do about this Ferrari situation?' He replied quite firmly, 'All I can tell you is that I think Ferrari will ruin your career'. Maybe not strictly true, but not many people have left Ferrari and gone on to greater things. Anyway, I didn't leave Ferrari, because I was under contract and that's all there

With Jo Siffert, my JW/Gulf Porsche team-mate, in the pits at Buenos Aires during practice for the 1971 Buenos Aires 1,000 km sports car race. We celebrated our first outing together with a win.

was to it. Lucien Bianchi shared the GT40 with Pedro at Le Mans and – you've guessed it – they won!

So time passed and after I left Ferrari in 1969 I wrote to Wyer asking him whether they would consider me for 1970. Back came a reply from David Yorke: 'We have no idea as to your current ability and therefore do not require you at the present time'. Or words to that effect.

So that was a nice kick in the teeth which rather brought me down to size, because I thought that John Wyer would jump at the chance of having me. But I'd done sweet nothing in 1969, so I suppose I should have realized. I didn't have any contact with the team again until 1970 after I'd driven Jacques Swaters's private Ferrari 512 at Spa, where I'd obviously impressed people. Then I did Le Mans in a factory Ferrari, which we'll come back to later, and suddenly David Yorke was hunting round. 'You are going very well. Well done lad, good boy,' that sort of thing.

Eventually, later on in the year, I was invited along to Goodwood to have a test run in a Porsche 917. They had also invited Ronnie Peterson and Peter Gethin, but I got the drive. Don't ask me why; I couldn't even tell you what sort of lap times we were doing!

So I was selected to join the team, but before I signed the contract I went up to Silverstone in October for another test run in the 917. When I got there it was raining, so they decided not to let me out in the 917, but asked me if I would have a run in their open Mirage

It was one of the worst racing cars I have ever driven.

which was fitted with the Gurney-Weslake V12 engine.

Well, obviously showing willing, I said 'that's fine' and took the damned thing out on to the track. I must admit it was one of the worst racing cars I have ever driven. It used to dart in every direction if it so much as ran over a seam on the tarmac. That day in the pouring rain hardly made things any better and I had a lot of spins.

As I was lapping I noticed John Wyer's Ford Mustang – registration number JW 500 – parked at various points round the circuit. The boss was obviously watching my progress. He was with a Dr Wylie, a senior engineer and a very important man within the Gulf organization, clearly showing him the team's new young driver at work. First I saw the car parked at Copse, then it moved down to Becketts and two laps later he was down at Woodcote.

So I'm thundering down the club straight towards them and brake for the corner. The Mirage starts shaking wildly under braking, but I still think 'Hell, I reckon I can brake even later than that next time round,' so I dive another 20 yards or so into the corner on my next lap. And the thing starts to spin!

It just spun like a top, round and round and round. I thought, 'Well, this really is it. I haven't signed the contract and there is John Wyer, sitting with one of the Gulf high rollers in his own personalized Ford Mustang, and his new hero is about to write them all off, along with his racing car. And push them all into the wall . . .'

However, on about the seventh spin, I saw a puff of smoke out of the corner of my eye as Wyer disappeared up the track out of my way. Thankfully, he still had the engine running. So I drove back to the pits while Wyer simply proceeded to drive out of the circuit, never bothering to come back to the pits.

When I pulled in, David Yorke was very reassuring. 'Don't worry lad,' he said, 'I saw it all'. I then got out and found that the car had nearly bald tyres on the rear wheels. I said, 'What on earth are you doing sending me out on stuff like that?' and he just shrugged and replied, 'Oh, we've sent off for the proper tyres now,' and off he went! Just amazing . . .

As far as this Mirage was concerned, they had the idea they might send me out to do some Can-Am races with it if it could lap Silverstone at a certain time. I was pretty keen to do more racing in the USA because it was a new and exciting experience at the time. So we ground round Silverstone for one entire day, getting nowhere really, until just before five o'clock in the afternoon I thought 'Oh, to hell with this,' and we just tightened up the roll bars and shock absorbers absolutely solid, making it feel just like a high-speed go-kart.

Off I went again, really flying. I passed a Formula 5000 car on my first lap, but there was always going to be the chance that I might brush one of those small bevelled kerbs which are on the inside edge of all the corners at Silverstone. Sure enough, gunning it through Club, I touched one of those kerbs and was almost history.

The bloody thing swapped ends in a split second and slammed straight into the wall. That was it. I was plastered from head to toe in boiling oil, but I staggered out of what was left of the car to see bits of debris scattered over 80 metres of road. Believe me, it was a *big* shunt!

Rather self-consciously, I found myself wandering up and down the track, picking up the pieces, trying to assemble them into something that still looked vaguely like a racing car! Of course, John Wyer had seen it all and absolved me of any blame. It was another case of 'Dear boy, I saw it all. Don't worry . . .' When we got back to the pits we found that the lap prior to my crash had been really quick, but the Mirage was just too nervous a proposition to consider racing seriously with any chance of success.

So that was the end of that idea. I never saw the car again, but some fellow I met told me he's acquired it and is using it in hill-climbs. He's very proud of the car. I just shudder when I think of it; I suppose if he's only driving it for 30 seconds at a time he can't frighten himself too often. It truly was an awful car!

Dear old John Wyer always looked very pallid and unwell. I think he'd been quite ill during his life and, after that glorious 1971 season with the Porsche 917, I think he was under quite a lot of pressure from the Gulf people to produce some more good results, so that couldn't have helped matters. But he was an enormously strong character. His organization and attention to detail in everything he did has stuck very firmly in my mind ever since.

In terms of professionalism, he was every bit the equal of how the Porsche works team is in the 1980s. I mean, you've only got to ask yourself why the Porsche factory asked Wyer to run his cars that season. He was totally meticulous. The team logged absolutely every detail of their cars' individual performance, long before this became the norm, even in Formula 1. By contrast, when I went to Surtees in 1974, they would keep my lap times on the back of a fag packet, or something similar! Wyer recorded everything and then had it neatly typed up on sheets to go into the files back at base.

I well recall testing with the 3-litre Mirages that we used after the Porsche year and Wyer would say to John Horsman, 'Don't you recall we had a problem rather like this with the GT40 at Reims back in 1968 . . .?' So they would consult the files, and there would be the answer.

In that respect it was an absolute delight to drive for them because the records so often provided a wonderful short-cut to solving technical queries. But I did feel rather like a school-kid and, make no mistake, you were severely reprimanded if things went wrong. I well remember at Le Mans in 1970 Mike Hailwood crashed one of the Gulf 917s in the wet. He came in to change tyres, found the pits already crowded, so they sent him back out again on slicks. He didn't make it and went off the road.

My relationship with Wyer was the first time I'd ever got really close to anybody in the professional racing world.

Eventually Hailwood got back to the pits on foot only for Wyer to fix him with a stare and say, 'Don't call us Mike, we'll call you'. He was a hard man to drive for. He would tell you precisely what he wanted, exactly what was required. He didn't suffer fools gladly; if he didn't like what was being said, he would just stop listening or even walk away. He was easily bored, but my relationship with him was enormously valuable. I suppose I had never really got to know the Ferrari engineers terribly well, so my relationship with Wyer was the first time I'd ever got really close to anybody in the professional racing world. I stayed with him for four more years after the 917 season, yet although in some ways I was his blue-eyed boy he always kept me at arm's length.

Since I stopped driving for John, I feel much closer to him than I ever did back in the 1970s, but I suppose that's quite natural. We're great friends, but in those days I got the strong impression that I was still a driver and, therefore, should be very much kept down in my rightful place!

The whole organization was extremely well structured, with David Yorke as Wyer's right-hand man and John Horsman in charge of the technical side. David was in charge of making sure that the drivers were in the right place at the right time, but there never seemed to be any panic, no flapping of any sort. David would just come up and say, 'Right, you're on in five minutes'. He also ensured that we were all fed and looked after, so he was a very important key person. Everybody had a great deal of respect for him.

John Horsman was a very talented and clever man. I think he was in absolutely the right position as the team's top dog on the engineering side when we ran those works Porsches. But when David Yorke went off to run the Martini Tecno deal (another story we'll come to in due course!), Horsman was left in total charge of the team, which wasn't such a good move in my view.

I've told him to his face and now I'll put it in black and white; I think this was a mistake. John just did not have the right temperament needed to handle the mechanics, to get the best out of them. The problem was that he was a super mechanic and engineer himself, but he couldn't stand back and delegate. He would just say, 'You're not doing it right, you're not doing it quick enough, so just get out of the way, you silly so-and-so'.

He just could not come to terms with the fact that he should have stood back and let the mechanics get on with it. He always had to be barging in there, wielding a spanner. I had a real argy-bargy with him coming back to England from Monza on one occasion and told John Wyer what I thought of the situation. The next thing I knew was that Horsman was phoning me up at home complaining that I'd been maligning him.

So I said, 'Look, I'm sorry John, but I just do not see how one man can do everything you've been trying to do'. For the life of me there was no way in which I could see him ensuring that John Wyer and his wife got their tickets and hotel reservations; making sure the mechanics were all right; checking that we'd got the new components, the right tyres; making sure that the drivers had their tickets, were in the right hotels and so on and so forth. It just wasn't feasible to do all these things. No way.

Sadly, John Horsman didn't understand my point of view and was really upset with me at the time. But in my honest opinion he was under intolerable pressure by 1972/73. After the Porsche era had finished, the Wyer team became part of the Gulf organization and we raced under the Gulf Research Racing banner so there was a great deal of pressure.

The 1972 season proved a difficult year for us, fielding the Mirage

M6 with its Cosworth DFV engine against the might of Ferrari and Matra. I shared the car with Gijs van Lennep, but we were not in the same class as the Italian and French cars. We were fourth at Spa, but my best result of the year was with Carlos Pace at Watkins Glen where I finished third. We didn't enter Le Mans, so I drove a Ferrari Daytona there, but that's another story we'll return to in the chapter about Le Mans.

During that tremendous 1971 season, Jo Siffert and I won the opening race in Buenos Aires, were second at Monza and Spa and third at Brands Hatch. Sadly Jo met his death at the wheel of a BRM P160 in the non-championship end-of-season Brands Hatch Formula 1 race. I also shared a 917 with Dickie Attwood to finish third at Watkins Glen, then took a second at Barcelona and won the Paris 1,000 km at Montlhéry, in both cases with van Lennep.

Looking thoughtful in the pits at Daytona during the 1971 24-hour classic. I had to wait another 15 years before scoring my first win in this event, which I came to believe is more demanding than Le Mans.

I developed an enormous affection for Jo, although I only did nine races with him before his death. But we spent a lot of time together and, largely I suspect because we had a similar outlook on life, got on very well indeed. Away from the cockpit he was a pleasantly relaxed sort of character who was game for an evening out, although not obviously on the night prior to a race. When we were testing at Daytona, for example, he would not be averse to slipping into one of the topless bars for a few beers with the mechanics just for a laugh. He was just good company.

You don't always strike up that sort of rapport with other drivers, but Siffert was definitely one of the easiest to get along with. I had a similar sort of relationship with Rolf Stommelen as well. On the track, of course, Siffert was a head-down, charging racing driver, always extremely competitive and totally desperate to beat Pedro Rodriguez, his arch-rival who drove the other Gulf Porsche 917.

I don't think Jo was disciplined at all.

Pedro and Jo came out of the same mould, but still somehow contrived to have different qualities. Pedro was much more controlled than Jo, who was a real charger. Yet when Pedro got down to it, he could charge harder than Jo at times. It was a strange contradiction.

When it came to self-discipline, I think Pedro was probably ahead. I don't think Jo was disciplined at all. He drove purely by the seat of his pants and was a truly great racing driver for all that. We used to discuss Formula 1 together quite often, because I was keen to get back into the swim of things in a Grand Prix car, and I always used to listen very attentively.

Jo's theory was that you should drive just about *any* Formula 1 car you could lay your hands on. I think I took that advice to heart and carried it too deep into my career, because I tended to drive any old dirt box that came in my direction, which I'm afraid was to my detriment. I don't think that philosophy is correct in the 1980s, but perhaps it was more valid during Jo's formative years. Anyway, I liked Jo, admired his driving and enjoyed his personality.

One thing I do particularly recall about Jo, though, was that he was quite hard on gearboxes. Back in 1971 Porsche used to blame me when we had gearbox problems, probably because I was the new boy in the team. Nothing too open, just the odd sniping remarks like, 'Ah, ze gearbox is not so good after ze race. You've damaged the gears, huh?'. I used to think, well, I'm sure I'm not hard on gearboxes, but all the same I began to wonder. And worry.

By the time we did the Watkins Glen 6-hours, poor Pedro was dead and I moved over to share what had been his 917 with Richard Attwood. Siffert was now driving with Gijs van Lennep and, during the course of the meeting Gijs came up to me and said, 'My God, the gearbox in that car is a real bloody mess'. So I pointed out that went to prove that it wasn't me who used to screw up the gearbox, but Jo – and I was getting the blame for it!

As far as Porsche was concerned, of course, Jo was highly rated. They had tremendous regard for him, perhaps more even than they did for Pedro. I suspect this was because Jo could speak German fluently, a little advantage which always helped slightly. I think if you speak the team's lingo, it obviously produces a slightly closer rapport with them. In fact, it sometimes surprises me that I've survived with Porsche for such a long time only speaking English.

Although the 1971 season with Porsche had helped me to establish a new reputation as a sports car driver, there was still that tantalizing lure of Formula 1 which I wasn't prepared to abandon. Consequently, when an exciting new chance to have a crack with a Grand Prix car for a full season looked as though it would come my way, I was over the moon with anticipation.

After the JW/Gulf Porsche programme came to an end, David Yorke parted company with the organization. I had got on extremely well with him, but always had the impression that he and John Wyer were not really compatible. Both rather highly strung, they were not what I would call calm people. But, to my mind, David was precisely the sort of person needed in the Gulf squad and, following on from my observations about John Horsman, I think we would have benefitted enormously if he had stayed with the team.

David moved to a new post as racing consultant to the Martini and Rossi organization, which had already been involved in backing the 917s entered by Porsche Salzburg. They liked his demeanour and retained him to advise on how they should tackle a Formula 1 involvement. Well, David suggested that they do a deal with the Brabham team, at that time right at the start of the Bernie Ecclestone era.

The idea was that I should join the team alongside Carlos Reutemann, so I really began to feel optimistic. At last I was going to get the full Grand Prix season I knew I needed in order to get the proper feel of the business. It looked like being an ideal arrangement which would, at last, salvage my hopes of a serious Grand Prix future. Then, out of the blue, the plans all changed. Luciano Pederzani, the boss man of Tecno, came in with what Martini and Rossi clearly assumed was going to be a Ferrari-beating deal. Tecno had forged a fine reputation as builders of F2 and F3 cars and now Pederzani had lavish ambitions for his new flat-12-engined Grand Prix car.

Martini and Rossi were tantalized; an Italian sponsor with an all-Italian car, out to take on Ferrari. Of course, how anybody in their senses could have believed they could do that is beyond me, but that was the ambition. I remember, very early in the development programme, talking to Count Gregorio Rossi about it. He said to me, 'You know, Derek, we'll be very pleased if we manage to get a third place by the end of the season'. I replied that they ought to count themselves lucky if the thing so much as qualified by the end of the year. I don't think they appreciated my pessimism!

The car was scheduled to be ready towards the end of November 1971, but a series of delays meant it did not get tested until just before Christmas. I was going to share it with the Italian driver Nanni Galli, and clearly I would not get a full season of Grands Prix the following year. So I went down to Turin, expecting to try the car the

My first acquaintance with the Formula 1 Tecno led me to believe that, perhaps, it might not be so bad after all. As things turned out, it was . . .

following morning, only to face yet another day of waiting while the car was completed.

Finally, the Tecno arrived at the Pirelli test track and, I must say, I was halfway impressed. They wheeled it out on to the tarmac, filled its cooling system with hot water, pressed the starter button and away she went. I had expected the engine to blow apart within half a mile, but it ran smoothly and sweetly all day.

David Yorke and I glanced at each other in disbelief. Perhaps it was going to work after all. I must say, I almost hoped it would be a disaster from the outset and that David would be able to persuade Martini that the Brabham deal was the answer after all. But, as I say, the engine ran all day and we were committed to it.

To be honest, that flat-12 sounded absolutely magic, but of course, we were just poodling up and down the straight at the Pirelli test track. We were not aiming at specific times at Imola or Monza, so no conclusions could be drawn.

Dwelling on my five races in the Tecno is a pretty painful experience! If readers want to know the complete, gruesome story, it can be found in the stark results sequence at the back of this volume. Suffice it here to say, it didn't add up to a great deal.

I drove the car at Clermont-Ferrand for the first time, practising for the '72 French Grand Prix. I adored that race track, having gone like a dream there in a 2-litre sports car race, so when I turned out for first practice I went quite well. But I never made any further progress.

Struggling with the Tecno in practice for the 1972 French Grand Prix. On race morning, several engine mounting bolts were found to be fractured, so I non-started the race.

We fiddled around with this and that, changing all the suspension settings, but nothing seemed to make any difference. Everybody else went quicker and quicker, while I went nowhere. Ultimately, I wound up last. Believe me, it was quite an eye-opener to drive!

On race morning, I arrived in the paddock to be met by David Yorke. 'Derek, you are not driving that car,' he said firmly. I said, 'How do you mean?'. We walked across to the pit lane where I was confronted with the sight of a mechanic at work with an oxy-acetylene torch, welding up the chassis.

It transpired that the flat-12 engine had been fitted as a stressed member and, throughout my practice runs, the securing bolts had been progressively snapping! That would have accounted for its strange handling, of course. I thing I'm right in recalling that four of the nine securing bolts on the backplate behind the cockpit had broken, so the Tecno was literally bending in the middle. That was the good bit; the programme went downhill from there!

For a young driver in my state, it was just about the last thing I needed at the time. As an intriguing tailpiece to the whole Tecno saga, I was told a most interesting story about those flat-12 engines only a couple of years ago, by somebody whose word I've always been inclined to trust. The rumour was that those engines were 'back door' jobs from Ferrari. Somebody smuggled out drawings of Maranello's flat-12s and that's how Tecno got the necessary know-how. It's a lovely tale, but one which, I suspect, we will never be able to confirm or deny.

Despite all these misfortunes, I was still determined to grasp any Formula 1 straw that came my way, and the next chance to present

Hopes that I might revive my Grand Prix career with some outings for Team Surtees in 1974 were to be sadly dashed. The TS16, seen here in the German Grand Prix at Nurburgring, proved a real handful and impossible to tame.

itself was a phone call from Louis Stanley at the end of the 1973 season. No, it wasn't an invitation for afternoon tea in his suite at the Dorchester, but asking me if I would like to test a BRM P160 at Silverstone.

It was the week following the Kyalami sports car race, after which I had planned to stay on and contest the Springbok series for 2-litre sports cars; staying in South Africa for two months was my idea of bliss. So I came back with the idea of returning to South Africa the following week, but it turned out that I had two days at Silverstone with the car and, as a result, didn't get back to South Africa.

Tim Schenken was also there for a test and the P160s were turned out in virgin white livery, the team's Marlboro deal having ended after the last race of the 1973 season. While the engine didn't have much punch, the chassis really felt quite nice and I remember I lapped quicker than Tim's best. Then Niki Lauda turned up and I equalled his time in my car, while being half a second slower than him in his own P160.

Despite a lot of chat from Big Lou, I didn't get the drive. He did a sponsorship deal with Motul, the French oil company, to take Jean-Pierre Beltoise, Henri Pescarolo and Francois Migault into the three-car line-up for 1974. I got the impression that Lou didn't really rate Niki Lauda very much, and since I was slightly slower than him, I suppose he thought I wasn't much use either. Then Niki went off to Ferrari, of course, and won the World Championship.

After a dismal handful of races with Team Surtees in 1974, my prospects of getting any further Formula 1 outings were absolutely rock-bottom and, as things turned out, 11th place in the German

Grand Prix at Nurburgring was my very last Grand Prix outing. Coincidentally, it was also the race in which dear old Mike Hailwood crashed his McLaren M23 and sustained injuries that ended his car racing career.

'For goodness sake, Derek, don't be so bloody serious about it all. Relax and enjoy yourself.'

Mike was a lovely bloke and, of course, plenty has been written by other people in praise of him. To be honest, our relationship was

Mike Hailwood's relaxed and philosophical attitude to motor racing was not something I could emulate, although I rather envied him for it. We raced together in the JW/Gulf Mirages, finishing fourth at Le Mans in 1974.

Throughout the early 1970s, the JW/Gulf Mirages were not really a match for the prototypes fielded by Matra and Ferrari. However, Ickx and I used one of them to win Le Mans in 1975, although by that time both the French and Italian teams had withdrawn from the sports car racing arena.

rather strange to start with; I didn't really warm to him when I first met him. He was quite a shy guy really, a bit on the casual side. But once I got to know him he was tremendous fun to be with. Up until his Nurburgring accident we were paired together in the Gulf Mirage team, winning at Spa and finishing fourth at Le Mans.

We got on very well, but I wasn't prepared to live it up in quite the way he did. I think after his bike racing, Mike's car racing was a fairly casual business. For me it was deadly serious and Mike was always saying 'For goodness sake, Derek, don't be so bloody serious about it all. Relax and enjoy yourself'. In some ways, I envied him that philosophy, but it wasn't really my way!

By the end of 1974, force of circumstances was taking me down the sports car route and I could sense that I was becoming tagged with that label. The following season was destined to produce my first win at Le Mans, sharing the Mirage with Jacky Ickx, but Gulf was limiting its programme to that one race, so I was free to accept an offer from Willi Kauhsen to drive his flat-12 cylinder Alfa Romeo TT3312s in those races that didn't clash.

Although Willi used to be a test driver at Porsche, I didn't really know him until, out of the blue, he rang up to ask whether I would like to be paired with Pescarolo for 1975.

I remember quite vividly going down to Paul Ricard for my first test. Truck after truck kept turning up, laden with more cars and equipment than you can believe. We had so many cars in the end that we just couldn't believe it. They had supposedly been set up by the factory, but closer examination indicated that there was still a fair deal of work to do. As an example, one of the rear wings was about half an inch higher on one side than on the other. It was so far out that it was obvious at a glance!

The mechanics were wonderful. I have always adored the Italians and their whole approach to motor racing, but my first outing behind the wheel of that Alfa convinced me it was a tank. You can't believe how awful it was to drive, but once Willi set to work, the whole project was quickly sorted out. It was great to see Kauhsen using his racing experience and engineering expertise to make them perform properly, even though I don't believe some of the works mechanics had ever heard of equipment like corner weights and only had the vaguest clue about toe-in and camber adjustments.

The engine, however, was just fantastic! You could rev the hell out of it. I remember little Art Merzario drove one of the other team cars and he was so tiny that his head just about poked above the steering wheel rim. I swear he never used the clutch at all; he used to whack that flat-12 up and down through the gearbox, giving it absolute hell. But it always used to struggle on to the finish, even with maybe half its valve springs broken. Pesca and I regularly revved them to 11,500 rpm and you could even risk it to 13,000 for short bursts. We had some good races.

The flat-12-engined Alfa Romeo didn't have much opposition in 1975 and we had an enjoyable season with the cars. You could rev them ferociously and they always seemed to hold together, even with several broken valve springs!

You spend a lot of time in sports car racing wondering just how good you really are.

I was particularly chuffed at Watkins Glen when I qualified my own car on pole position and, effectively, took second place in the spare.

Right *The Lotus Seven which I shared with John Penfold during my first season of racing in 1964.*

Right and below *On the grid at Silverstone and Goodwood with our Lotus 31. Bought with a BMC engine installed, we soon replaced that with a home-brewed Ford unit built by John Upton round standard bits bought from a local Ford dealer and fitted with a Cosworth cylinder head. With this car I briefly held the F3 record at Goodwood, beating Jackie Stewart's 1964 best with the Tyrrell Cooper-BMC.*

Above *Felday family group at Zolder in 1967, prior to my winning the Coupe de l'Avenir in the Brabham BT21. From left to right: Sue Westbury, Mick Earle, Jim Charman, Geoff Evans, Pam, myself, Mac Daghorn and Peter Westbury.*

Right *That wonderful Tasman Dino 246, a real jewel of a racing car, during the splendid 1969 series in Australia and New Zealand where I partnered Chris Amon in a works-supported effort.*

Not so wonderful! Back for the Tasman series a year later, at the end of 1970, with the ex-works Wheatcroft Brabham BT26. I finished second in the New Zealand Grand Prix with it before Chris Amon blew its one remaining engine trying to sort out the handling for me. It had been designed to run on Goodyears and I could never make it work on the Dunlops we used down under!

Left *On the rostrum with Jo Siffert after my first major international win, the 1971 Buenos Aires 1,000 km with the Gulf Porsche 917. Standing in front of us are Pedro Rodriguez and Jackie Oliver, who shared the second Gulf Porsche entry. The crowds really join in the spirit of things in South America!*

Right *Heavy metal! I lead the opening stages of the 1977 Nurburgring round of the European Touring Car Championship in the massive 5.3-litre V12 Broadspeed-prepared Jaguar XJC. Andy Rouse and I finished second behind the BMW coupé driven by Gunnar Nilsson and Dieter Quester.*

The Jules-sponsored factory Porsche 936 which helped my dream come true! It certainly ran like one at Le Mans in 1981, where I shared the run to victory with Jacky Ickx, our second triumph together at the Sarthe.

Inset *Norbert Singer cleans my vizor: there was precious little else to do, apart from topping up the fuel, as the car ran like a clock.*

Left *A heartening sight! In amongst the sea of spectators at Le Mans in 1983, a Union Jack highlights a group of DB supporters!*

What made it all the more satisfying was that I was quicker than Mario Andretti who had joined the team for this race. That was important to me, because I wasn't in Formula 1 any more and you spend a lot of time in sports car racing wondering just how good you really are. You don't often come up against a great driver like that, so it was gratifying to have out-qualified him.

To be honest, though, throughout the season I kept thinking to myself, 'Well, this is all very well, but who on earth are we beating?'. The super-high-technology Renault turbos kept setting the pace and then falling out, after which there was nothing to beat but the other Alfas, so I always used to come away from the races taking my successes with a pinch of salt because we were really the only ones who could win anyway.

That said, I got quite a kick from winning at Spa where I beat Jacky Ickx fair and square on his home ground in the same car. He drove one of the Alfas in that race and I remember the battle I had trying to get past him. It was wet, yet again, and as we hurtled down through Eau Rouge and up through Raidillon, I was right on his tail, catching him all the way.

As we went up the long hill, Jacky would move from one side to the other, just enough to make it too difficult for me to overtake. Of course, when the track is still wet, it's very tricky when you get off the dry racing line, but eventually I just came through Eau Rouge so much faster than him and barged my way past going up the hill.

I went on to win the race, but I never got much publicity for that. Amazing, really; if Ickx had won, it would have been 'Spa rain master wins again!', but in fact I had beaten him in the rain in a straight fight, so everybody assumed there had to be a hidden reason for him not winning. Afterwards, Jacky sidled up to me and said, with a grin, 'It's amazing how narrow that track seems . . .'

Willi Kauhsen stands between Henri Pescarolo and myself after Pesca and I had won the 1975 Spa 1,000 km race in one of his team's Alfa Romeo T33TT12s. Willi and his crew did a fine job sorting out the Italian cars which won the World Sports Car Championship that season.

Kicking up the spray at Spa in the winning Alfa, shortly after elbowing my way past Jacky Ickx's sister car. I rated that achievement – beating Ickx in the wet on his own patch – as one of my better races.

Frankly, I've suffered a lot of that in my career and I don't think I've been respected as being a good rain driver. More recently, in the works Porsche team, I've heard people say on a rainy morning, 'Good job Hans Stuck's here because it's wet'. But, in fact, I'm invariably almost as quick as Stuck in the wet and he'll admit it. I think in many ways I may have suffered slightly being paired with these two drivers, both of whom have incredible flair. But the fact remains that I'm much quicker in the rain, relatively speaking, than I am in the dry.

Jacky could drive *anything* well.

I think this is an appropriate time to mention Jacky Ickx in more detail. I won my first three Le Mans victories with him and I believe we developed a special relationship, possibly better than any other driver has enjoyed with him. Long before we drove together I always had a great deal of respect for him. In my days at Ferrari he was one of the sport's rising stars, obviously terribly, terribly talented and, on his retirement in 1985, the world's most versatile racing driver without a doubt.

Jacky could drive *anything* well and had the most amazing ability to turn on the pressure just when it was needed. I admired his professionalism, the way he drove on the day and, when he and I competed together, I like to think that he felt the same about me.

Whenever I took over a car from Jacky, it was never any worse than it had been when I handed it over to him. Part of our success together must have stemmed from the fact that we drove in very similar styles. One thing that does annoy me slightly in connection with Jacky is the way that many people regard him as just a good sports car driver. They forget that he was an absolutely brilliant Grand Prix driver in his heyday, and considered by some to be the very best in the world. He was an Ayrton Senna of his time, a man who was going all the way. Talking of him purely as a man who has won Le Mans six times tends to devalue his achievements. People should not forget that.

After the Alfas, the next thing on the agenda for the mid-1970s was the Jaguar programme with the big 5.3-litre V12-engined XJ coupés. I was contracted at the start of 1976, but we didn't get the thing out and racing until the Silverstone Tourist Trophy at the end of the season and the full racing programme was delayed until the following year. It was a fiasco from start to finish, highlighting what was in my opinion a very fundamental lack of communication between the PR department of Jaguar and dear old Ralph Broad, whose Broadspeed operation prepared the cars for Leyland and was put in a

A busy day testing at Goodwood in 1976 in the Mirage which Vern Schuppan and I were destined to take to fifth place at Le Mans. By now Gulf had pulled out and the cars were owned by Harley Cluxton and entered under his GTC (Grand Touring Cars) banner. My friend and neighbour David Purley was also testing his F5000 Chevron that day, and other associates in this shot include John Horsman (with camera, immediately to the left of my helmeted head) and Mick Earle (in white shirt just behind the Mirage's left rear wing end plate).

rather helpless position.

It was a telephone call from Simon Pearson, one of the PR guys at Leyland, that first got me involved with the project. I went up to have lunch with him and thought the idea sounded great. I had always wanted to drive a British car in a serious international racing effort, but the whole plan misfired very badly from the start.

The project was unveiled in London in April, amidst a great fanfare and fuss. The curtains swept back to reveal the whole team, and then one of the Leyland spokesmen stepped forward and said 'Ladies and gentlemen, this is the car with which we are going to win the European Touring Car Championship round at the Salzburgring in three weeks . . .'. My jaw just fell open. The car hadn't turned a wheel at this stage and here was this guy talking about winning races!

To be brutally frank, Leyland just had not got a clue about the realities involved behind the development of a racing programme. David Hobbs and I, who had also been signed to drive, just looked at each other, knowing there was no way. But the damage had been done; many of the press brigade went away thinking, 'This is it! Here we go with the big British hope. Bang, bang, bang . . .'.

Of course, what Jaguar *should* have said at that point was 'This is the car with which we are going to contest the European Touring Car Championship when we feel it has been developed to a competitive pitch'. Then everybody would have said fine, good luck. The press could have been told how testing was going and that would have been it, a balanced and well thought-out programme. But, no. They tell everybody how good it is going to be, and while I'm sure the specialist motor sporting press went away shaking their heads, thinking, 'Oh my Lord, not again,' just like we drivers were, the national press was thinking, 'Great, this is the Jaguar that's going to beat the world'. Then, of course, when it didn't happen . . .

There were just so many things wrong with the car that I am hard pressed to recall them in the correct sequence. But basically it was pretty normal for the rear axle to overheat, the brakes wouldn't work properly and the engine suffered from dramatic oil surge problems. It doesn't really matter which came first. The brakes used to overheat dramatically, but that didn't always matter too much because by then the oil surge would damage the bearings and, in turn, by the time they had solved both these problems the differential would fail because it couldn't stand up to the pace.

It was just one thing after another. I remember testing at Goodwood on one occasion when suddenly this wheel went racing past me, disappeared over the bank, and it took us about an hour to find it. Thankfully, I managed to keep the car under control and came to rest without hitting anything hard!

Eventually we turned up at the Silverstone Tourist Trophy at the end of the year. I got pole position and we led the race. I drove the first stint, but I just knew it wasn't going to last the distance because the brakes just wouldn't take it. I eventually handed it over to Hobbo and, of course, he had a wheel come off the thing. It was a terrible let down for all of us, not to mention the enormous crowd which had turned up to watch the Jaguar take on the BMWs. When I drove it round to take our place on the grid, everyone in the grandstand just stood up and cheered. It was great to get that sort of response from the public, but all the more frustrating to let them down so badly.

So our 'victory at the Salzburgring' dwindled into pole position and fastest lap at Silverstone. None the less, we looked forward to 1977, only for that to turn into a giant Leyland corporate cock-up as well.

The full racing programme got off on the wrong foot because Jaguar would not finalize the decision whether to continue racing or not. There were four drivers – Andy Rouse, Tim Schenken, John Fitzpatrick and myself – all wondering whether we should hang on for a decision or go off to see if they could fix up drives in other teams. And, most importantly, Ralph Broad's guys didn't know whether to get on with their development programme, because they were going to need bigger wheels to accommodate bigger brakes for 1977, which naturally was going to involve major chassis and suspension alterations.

Eventually I just had to ring up the company's director of sales and marketing, Keith Hopkins, and finally went to see him in the Leyland lounge at the Motor Show. I said, 'Look, I've just got to confront you with this. There are four drivers all waiting, Broadspeed is waiting and none of us knows what we're supposed to be doing. You can't just say, "OK, great, let's go motor racing," and expect the car to be ready. The decision should have been made as early as September, preferably sorting out a three-year programme in order that some long-term planning could take place. You can't produce a new competition car simply by flicking a light switch. It doesn't happen that way.'

I rate Andy as one of the best saloon car drivers in the business.

I think I got the point across, but it was not until the end of November that they said, right, we'll be racing again next year. Not that there were any decent results coming our way in 1977; the only race we finished without trouble was the Nurburgring where Andy Rouse and I took second place.

I rate Andy as one of the best saloon car drivers in the business; he really is outstandingly good. So we turned up at the Nurburgring to be confronted by the entire German press corps telling us, 'Ah, zat is a very big car. No vay to beat ze BMW here, you know'. Publicly, I said, 'Well, let's wait and see,' but privately Andy, myself and the whole team basically knew that viewpoint was correct. It was the hardest track of the season from the car's point of view, so it was ironic that in the one race where we should have run from the start content to stay behind the leading BMW that the Jaguar should last out. We finished second.

Afterwards, I remember going up to the victory circle and being congratulated by Eddie Guba, one of Germany's most respected racing journalists. Eddie said, 'Vell done, that's very good!'. I replied, 'No Eddie, it isn't. Second place is not the same as winning'. And of course he came back with the inevitable 'Ha! Ve ver second once – look vere ve are now!' That's been one of my standard motor racing after-dinner talk stories ever since!

Eddie said, 'Vell done, that's very good!' I replied, 'No Eddie, it isn't. Second place is not the same as winning'.

Back at the Tourist Trophy we were running second in the closing stages of the race, but Andy threw it into the wall as he tried to make up ground on the leading BMW coupé. I understand how hard he was driving, but I honestly don't believe that any professional driver is paid to stick the car off the road nine laps from the finish. Basically, I reckon at that stage of a long-distance race it is better to finish second than crash the car. I don't say I wouldn't have been trying hard myself, but I suppose my feeling is based on the fact that I have

Putting a brave face on it! Joking with fellow team drivers Tim Schenken and John Fitzpatrick, while BMS CSL ace Gunnar Nilsson (left, in overalls) listens intently.

This is the Alpina BMW CSL which I shared with Harald Ertl to win the 1973 Tourist Trophy at Silverstone. Three years later I returned with the first of the Broadspeed-prepared Leyland Jaguar XJCs which, although I started from pole position, still had to give best to the German cars!

Three-wheeling the big Jag during the European Touring Car Championship event at Brno, in Czechoslovakia. They were quick enough, but lacked development and were mechanically too frail.

been extremely fortunate throughout my career not to bend too many cars. Andy should have tempered that enthusiasm to win with a little more control.

There was a peculiar twist to that result, of course, because the eventual winner we were chasing was Tom Walkinshaw in a BMW CSL coupé. He later went on to mastermind the Jaguar's motor racing revival in the early 1980s and his team's Jaguar V12 sports cars became the biggest thorn in the side of our Porsche factory effort from 1986 onwards.

Having won the Tourist Trophy myself four years earlier, sharing an Alpina CSL with the late Harald Ertl, I would really love to have repeated the achievement in a Jaguar. But by the time the XJ coupés returned for that second TT outing the writing was on the wall and I think the whole team realized the programme would not be continuing into 1978. They were big, brutish cars, but *tremendously* fast, capable of pulling around 170 mph on the straight at Brno, for example. It was a shame their reliability was so dreadful.

I must say, 1977 produced a very mixed bag of racing for me. In addition to the Jaguar project, I was trying to retain some sort of identity as a single-seater driver by driving a Penske PC3, owned by Hexagon of Highgate, in the domestic British Formula 1 series, and at the other end of the scale received an invitation to drive for Renault at Le Mans.

In 1977 I used this ex-works Formula 1 Penske PC3 for several outings in the domestic British F1 series, the highlight of which was winning the Gold Cup at Oulton Park. The car was owned by Paul Michaels, boss of Hexagon of Highgate, the specialist sports car dealers.

Gerard Larrousse asked me to drive for the team and I'll deal with our race performances in the chapter about Le Mans itself. They shaped up well as a racing organization and I enjoyed working for them. At that time there was an infectious air of youthful enthusiasm breezing through the whole outfit. By contrast, I had always felt Porsche's attitude was 'Oh, we've done this all before. Let's roll the car out, shake the dust off and see if we can blow the opposition away'. Really, they gave the impression of being rather complacent.

I had always felt Porsche's attitude was 'Oh, we've done this all before'.

There was a real buzz being a part of this young, highly motivated bunch of people, working with engineers like Michel Tetu, who later designed the Renault Grand Prix cars and now works with the Ligier team. Bernard Dudot, who masterminded the team's engine programme, was also a great inspiration behind everybody's efforts.

I shared with Jean-Pierre Jabouille in 1977, then returned to drive with Jean-Pierre Jarier the following year, when the team won with the Jaussaud/Pironi car. Mine failed to finish on both occasions, but I was the only non-French driver in the line-up for those two Le Mans outings. I was immensely flattered that my efforts at winning Le Mans in 1975 earned me such a compliment from Larrousse and the Renault Sport management.

To be truthful, by the end of the 1970s, I began to think that my professional racing career, along with a lot of other people's, was falling apart. Sports cars had got into a terrible mess thanks to the introduction by the sport's governing body of the Group 5 silhouette regulations which nobody really wanted. The only people interested were Porsche, who already had the rocket-like Turbo Carrera, so they won just about everything, apart from at Le Mans where you were still allowed to run Group 6 prototypes like the Renault.

Throughout the 1970s, I suppose my income from racing must have been between ten and twelve thousand pounds a year.

Scratching around Silverstone in the lumbering Aston Martin which David Preece trundled to last place in the 1979 6-hours. This was a typically frustrating period of my career when no top drives seemed to come my way.

Throughout this time I was struggling hard to make a reasonable living as a professional racing driver. As far as I was concerned, if I could generate a basic income, I knew I could live through the year on it, pay for the cost of the kids growing up and do what I wanted to do. We had a lovely house, on the beach, near Bognor, but while people thought I was some sort of millionaire, we had bought it for about £21,000 in 1971 and, throughout the 1970s, I suppose my income from racing must have been between ten and twelve

At work at home. Struggling with the restoration of an old smugglers' boat which has been cleverly converted into a small cottage in the grounds of our home at Pagham.

thousand pounds a year. During that period I was steadily getting deeper and deeper in debt with the bank. I felt a long way from being a millionaire, I can assure you of that.

Then, in 1981, we got the chance to buy Little Welbourne, our current home, which I had always hankered to live in ever since I was a kid. The retired gentleman who lived there before us wanted a home on the beach with a smaller plot that would require less upkeep, so we effectively swapped houses, with my paying him a financial adjustment. It's an absolutely lovely place to call home, overlooking Pagham harbour, and I aim to spend the rest of my days here. It will see me out.

However, the new house was one hell of a commitment and, frankly, I'm still up to my eyeballs in it. Thankfully, my career was on the verge of taking another turn for the better as I began to forge a new, long-term relationship with the manufacturer for whom I would eventually win two World Championships and four more Le Mans victories.

My days as a regular member of the Porsche factory sports car team were about to get off the ground.

Chapter 3

Porsche: a special partnership

At the wheel of the superb JW/Gulf Porsche 917 speeding to second place in the 1971 Spa 1,000 km, sharing, as usual, with Jo Siffert.

IT MAY seem slightly surprising, but I did not really have a great deal of direct contact with the Porsche factory personnel during my season driving the JW/Gulf 917s in 1971. Mostly I dealt with John Wyer and David Yorke who, in turn, liaised with the Porsche management. However, I do recall being asked out to Hockenheim to test a 917 before the winter closed in. They needed to evaluate some differing bodywork configurations, which were particularly important for Le Mans, before the start of the racing season and I was the one selected for the job.

It was a great feeling to be summoned there and realize you were part of something as important as the Porsche factory team. Aside from that rather fragmented and uncertain time with Ferrari, it was my first experience of being a works driver. I felt tremendous elation, mixed with optimism and confidence. Perhaps in my last seven seasons as a member of the Rothmans Porsche squad, I have unconsciously slipped into taking that all for granted. But I can guarantee the moment you are no longer in a works team its real benefits suddenly become starkly apparent!

So I was asked out to Hockenheim where we tested using the old circuit, without the chicanes or the infield stadium loop. Just the 'perimeter track', so to speak. It meant hurtling straight into the stadium section flat-out, ignoring the tricky right-hander I was so familiar with from my Formula 2 outings there. The weather was awful and much of the circuit was pretty slippery by any standards.

Nipping through the Esses during the early stages of the 1971 Le Mans 24-hour classic with the special long-tailed Porsche 917 which proved very quick, but unreliable. During winter tests to evaluate this bodywork at Hockenheim I almost accounted for an extremely audacious local cyclist!

I didn't fly out from England until the morning of the test, so by the time I arrived at Hockenheim Herbert Linge was going round doing some television work, so I didn't get my backside into the car until after lunch. At that point, I discovered that they expected me to test about five different rear bodywork configurations! Even though it was now teeming with rain and coming over foggy, the work had to be completed, come what may. They did not anticipate being able to test again until well into the New Year, probably as late as February, so we just had to press on and finish the programme, however long it took.

I remember that the 917 had its passenger seat absolutely stacked with computerized material and, at a certain point on the fast return straight, I had to flick a switch to trip a beam which relayed

information to the computer, then flick the switch back off, while at the same time scrambling into the stadium, hoping that I was going to keep the car on the road.

To cut a long story short, I tested all these body configurations, some of which were quicker on the straight at the expense of the downforce in the corners, some good in the corners but not so fast in a straight line. To be honest, I reckon that the long-tailed Le Mans bodywork was probably producing about the same lap times as the conventional, shorter tails, but I was never really certain because the conditions were so horribly wet and murky. It took about 40 minutes to change the bodywork, so by the end of the day I was just squeezing in a single lap at a time as it was rapidly getting dark.

Just before the end of the afternoon, I was flying up the straight leading into the stadium with the headlights on, running at around 170 mph in the dusk, when the beam picked out a sight so unbelievable that, for a split second, I thought I was hallucinating. There was a bloke cycling across the road, as cool as you like!

The sheer panic written all over his face has stayed in my mind ever since.

I just remember seeing his horror-stricken face – obviously it was his short-cut home through the woods at five o'clock and here he was, suddenly confronted by this Porsche 917 thundering towards him at 170 mph. At that speed, I just dared not swerve a fraction, so I missed him by what seemed like the width of a cigarette paper. The sheer panic written all over his face was something that has stayed in my mind ever since.

At the end of the tests, I got back to the Porsche truck in the paddock in time to watch Norbert Singer, the chief of the racing development department, unravel all the rolls of computer graph paper which he then studied intensely for a long time. It was just about the first time I had met him, so I was looking over his shoulder trying to follow what he was saying, although, to be honest, I didn't have much of a clue.

Eventually Norbert ended up with piles of paper all over the place, but finally got round to comparing two read-outs with what looked to me like wildly dissimilar results. To my untrained eye there was a hell of a difference between the two read-outs, about six inches of variation on the paper.

'That's an enormous difference, there!' I chimed in, trying to be helpful. 'Oh no it isn't,' he replied and then proceeded to take out his slide rule and prove that a difference of something like one-tenth of a second showed up like six inches on the read-out. Anyway, I must confess that I was hard-pressed to see the point of it all in those diabolical conditions, but that was my first serious encounter with the

Porsche factory's way of working. It was a taste of things to come.

I suppose the next time that I really got involved with them was at the 1971 Le Mans test weekend, where the 917s were being tried with the long enclosed tail sections that I had first used in the wet at Hockenheim. At one point I came into the pits and Norbert asked me what revs I was pulling on the Mulsanne Straight. I said '8,100 rpm'. He replied, 'Ah, that is very good. At 8,200 rpm, the engine blows up'.

It amounted to 246 mph on the Mulsanne straight.

With that, he began to do some complex calculations on his slide rule. Then he grunted, laughed out loud and walked away. I chased after him to ask what it was all about. He replied, 'I've just calculated what 8,100 rpm equates to in top gear, allowing for tyre growth'. He added that it was probably better that I didn't know. So I said, 'Look, Jo Siffert and I have got to drive that thing for 24 hours. It would be nice to know what we are letting ourselves in for'. So he told me. It amounted to 396 kph – 246 mph – on the Mulsanne straight. We've never been as quickly down there since!

Ironically, all the trick-bodied 917s fell out during the night, leaving Helmut Marko and Gijs van Lennep to win with a regular 917K entered by the Martini team. The long-tailed cars were hampered by grease blowing out of their rear hubs, but what eventually put Siffert and me out was a slight oil leak, although we had run very quickly indeed during the early stages.

Once my season with the JW/Gulf 917s was over, I had no more contact with Porsche for five years. I heard nothing from them until 1976 after I finished fifth at Le Mans, sharing a Mirage with Vern Schuppan. They rang me and asked whether I would drive the Kremer team's Porsche 935 in the Austrian 1,000 km race at the Osterreichring. Obviously Kremer was one of the favoured Porsche privateers and the factory gave them quite a lot of assistance and encouragement. Anyway, I went down and drove it, again with Vern, and we finished fourth. I suppose you could say that represented my informal 'reinstatement' to the Porsche ranks. For the next couple of years they approached me repeatedly to drive for them at Le Mans, but of course I became involved with Renault and really wanted to stick with the French team, enjoying their enthusiasm and hell-for-leather lack of any inhibitions. So I drove the Renaults for two years, followed by Harley Cluxton's Mirage in 1979, before Porsche asked me *again* whether I would be keen to drive there in 1980. Frankly, I was happy to do so, because there were not too many offers coming my way at around that time.

Porsche was entering a trio of 924 Carrera GTs in the race, cars

The Porsche 934s and 935s were never exactly my favourite cars, being real handfuls to drive close to the limit. Here I am in one of Georg Loos's cars working hard during the 1977 Nurburgring 1,000 km.

intended to form the basis of the factory's Group B development, and I was asked to share one with Andy Rouse and Tony Dron, entered by Porsche GB. In the event, I got swapped around to share with Al Holbert, who I had never met before, in one of the other entries.

My official return to the Porsche fold, at Le Mans, was a warming experience.

From the outset, it was obvious we had no chance of winning overall, but my official return to the Porsche fold, at Le Mans, was a warming experience which I valued enormously. I could sense that it would help my career at yet another crucial turning point. By eight o'clock on the Sunday morning, we had got up to fifth place in a little 2-litre car with 320 bhp. I think that made a great deal of difference to my future with the works team.

Unfortunately, burnt valves caused us to fade to 13th at the finish, the last of the Carrera GTs to take the flag, but I knew I had made a major point. Porsche was obviously impressed by the way things had gone because they asked me to drive again the following year on the same basis. But I felt I just couldn't drive the small-capacity car again.

I wrote back and said, 'No way, I'm sorry. But thank you very much for letting me drive the Carrera GT in the last race'. Do you know, I believe that this was the first time I'd ever written to a team thanking them for letting me drive? That's awful, really, but you usually do a deal at the start of the season, shake hands on it, and that's it. Happily, I don't think I've ever fallen out with anybody because of that, but perhaps it's something that everybody should bear in mind. Anyway, by the end of 1980, I knew I just couldn't face driving a small-capacity car again. If I ran at Le Mans, I wanted something good.

Another problem was that I couldn't guarantee getting an offer from Porsche for any other races, so that posed something of a sticking point. I was being offered drives from other teams to run a complete programme, with Le Mans thrown in, yet I knew that obviously a works Porsche drive was going to give me the best chance there. If it came up. But, on the other hand, I could hardly turn down every other sports car racing offer just for the sake of a single race. The mortgage still had to be paid!

Then, out of the blue, I received an offer. It came from Steve O'Rourke, manager of the Pink Floyd pop group, who is a tremendous motor racing enthusiast. At the same time I was really pushing for a place with either the Kremer or the Georg Loos private Porsche teams, but I found it rather a difficult business. I hate selling

Preparing for the 1980 Le Mans effort. I test one of the Porsche 924 Carrera GTs at Paul Ricard prior to my first outing at the Sarthe in a true factory Porsche entry. Sharing with Al Holbert, I was to get up to fourth at one point before the exhaust valves began to burn out.

myself. Somehow, it seems so demeaning, always ringing people up, bothering them for drives. I hate getting the, 'Oh yes, we're looking for drivers, we'll let you know, ring us next week' type of brush-off. In my view, if people want you, they get in contact and ask. It's as simple as that. If they don't, then you hear nothing from them.

> I hate selling myself. Somehow, it seems so demeaning.

However, in this particular case, Steve was setting up a programme for 1981 and offered me eight races, including Le Mans. He was toying with the idea of getting a private Lancia but I talked him out of that one. I figured any private team wasn't going to get parity of equipment with the works Martini cars, so I suggested he buy a BMW M1 coupé.

We went down to Munich to talk it over with Dieter Stappert, then BMW's competition manager, and he was very positive. Yes, they would help us out with spares and back-up, but I was still very conscious of the fact that I was part of a private team. I got the feeling we were being treated quite casually by BMW, even though we were customers. A case of 'come down next Monday' and when you arrived it was 'Oh, we forgot you were coming'. That sort of stuff really peeves me. I don't want to be treated like a king, but it was a bit rich getting that sort of response when we had traipsed all the way to Munich for a specific meeting! At the end of the day everything worked out pretty well, and we duly got the car, one of the old Pro-cars which had been used by several Grand Prix drivers the previous season.

Just prior to our first race at Monza, I suddenly read in the motor racing press that Porsche were going to enter a trio of 936s at Le Mans. My first reaction wasn't even to be disappointed. I just thought 'Well, damn my luck,' but that was the end of it. Jacky Ickx, Bob Wollek, Rolf Stommelen, Jochen Mass . . . they were all part of the Porsche line-up, but I just shoved it out of my mind and got on with the BMW programme.

So down to Monza I go with Steve O'Rourke, check into the Hotel de Ville just down the road from the circuit and who should I bump into but Valentin Schaeffer, one of Porsche's senior engine men. He came up and asked me what I was doing there. I told him and he replied, 'Ah, why don't you drive for us at Le Mans this year?' I explained that I couldn't because I was already committed to this BMW. 'Pity,' he said, 'because we still require another driver', implying that there might still be a place for me.

At that, I began to prick up my ears. 'Surely you've got all your drivers sorted out?' But Valentin tipped me the wink that they were not all finalized by that stage. It wasn't really anything to do with him, of course, but he had his ear firmly to the ground and knew everything that was going on.

Later that evening, over dinner, Steve asked me who Schaeffer was. I explained everything that Valentin had said to me, the entire story. Immediately Steve said, 'Derek, if Porsche want you, I would really be flattered to release you to drive for them. If they want my driver, then I would be prepared to let you go'. My mouth must have fallen open on the spot. I enjoyed my meal, then went to bed and could hardly sleep all night. I just lay in bed and thought. Now I know this may sound excruciatingly corny, but I honestly had a premonition. That night I *knew* I was going to win Le Mans. I didn't know who I was going to drive with, but I knew I would win. I just couldn't get to sleep, thinking about it.

I honestly had a premonition. That night I *knew* I was going to win Le Mans.

In the pit lane the following morning Steve O'Rourke came back to me and said, 'Look, thinking about last night, I'm not sure I really can release you. I'm sorry, but I need you at Le Mans too much'. So I said, 'Well, Steve, as a matter of fact, I've already invited you to the victory party. Anyway, I've already told Manfred Jantke at Porsche that I'm available'. He said, 'You didn't – did you?' So I came clean and said, 'No, not really. As a matter of fact I haven't. But I'm just about to . . .'

'Now we have the two best drivers in the business—you and Jacky Ickx.'

So Steve thought about it for a moment and said, 'Right, if they make you a firm offer, come back and we'll discuss it'. The BMW retired at Monza with electrical problems, so I flew straight home and spoke to Jantke on the phone the following morning. I had to play things very carefully, not wanting to lose the O'Rourke deal if I couldn't get the Porsche one. But Jantke amazed me by saying, 'The drive is yours. Now we have the two best drivers in the business – you and Jacky Ickx. You will drive with him'.

I just couldn't believe it. I mean, I thought I might get a chance in the second car, but not with Jacky. So I told Manfred that I now had to go back and diplomatically get out of a drive which had offered me a whole season's income.

I rang up Steve O'Rourke on some lame pretext about getting hold of some video tapes he had promised me; I just didn't figure I could

*My trip to Le Mans in 1980 was originally intended to be behind the wheel of this Michael Cane Racing ex-Procar series BMW M1. I had already finished second in the Silverstone 1,000 km with David Hobbs and Steve O'Rourke (**right**, on rostrum) and it was only through Steve's matchless generosity that I was released from my contract and thus allowed to accept that crucial invitation from Porsche.*

raise the subject of Le Mans with him on the phone. He said, sure, pick them up from the office tomorrow. So, next morning, Pam and I went up to London and dropped into Steve's office. 'Can we see Steve O'Rourke, please?'

His secretary explained that he was busy, so I trotted out the inane business about how he was going to leave me a couple of tapes. OK, so we came back later. By then Steve had gone out to lunch, 'But he's left you the tapes. Here they are'. At this point I had to come clean, effectively saying, 'Look, I don't actually want the tapes, I want to see Steve'. So eventually I went back a third time, saw Steve and he agreed to discuss it with Michael Cane, his team manager.

It transpired that they immediately contacted BMW's Competitions Manager Dieter Stappert who said, 'You've just got to release Derek. It's too big an opportunity for him to miss. He could win the race in a Porsche. He's not about to do that in an M1'. Once Steve was assured that he would still get some support from BMW, the way was clear for me to drive the Jules-sponsored 936 at Le Mans.

I never saw the car until it was rolled out of the truck at Le Mans. Within four laps of sitting in it for the first time I had gone quicker than I had ever managed round Le Mans before. The rest is just history. They never took a body panel off for the entire 24 hours. They just topped up the oil through the external filler and it didn't miss a beat. We flew the whole way. It was simply unbelievable.

There it was. My second Le Mans victory. Porsche's chief executive Peter Schutz said to me, 'Derek, next year we are going to run a full programme of Group C racing. We hope you will be part of it and contribute a great deal of input into the operation'. That was the moment I knew I was away, up and running with Porsche for what you might call the long haul.

None of it would have been possible without Steve O'Rourke and his generosity.

Yet none of it would have been possible without Steve O'Rourke and his generosity, his humanity. If I had not been in a position to grab that opportunity with Porsche, then I honestly believe that somebody else would have got the break and I would have been history. My career would never have developed along the lines it subsequently did and I'm pretty certain that this book would never have been written!

When I became involved with Porsche more closely, I discovered that this rather casual we've-done-it-all-before approach is something of an illusion. Everything the company does is very precise and considered. They spend a lot of time mulling over detail changes and every time any of the cars were rolled out of the transporter you

Fuel stop for the 1981 Le Mans-winning Porsche 936 which I shared with Jacky Ickx to score our second such success together. It was the victory which set the seal on my future as a full-time member of the factory Porsche team from 1982 onwards.

could rely on them having any number of subtle technical tweaks under the skin. They might not be obvious changes that everybody was aware of, but there was constant development going on behind the scenes, on engines, transmissions, electronics and fuel systems. Just about every aspect of the car you could think of.

As I've said before, I opted for Renault in 1977 and '78 because their personnel seemed more youthful, enthusiastic and motivated. Porsche seemed to epitomize the establishment and the whole business of racing did not seem like such a great challenge to them. Only when I joined them did I start to appreciate how incorrect I had been in that appraisal.

Joining Porsche opened my eyes in a big way. The sheer scale of the whole operation never fails to impress me. They have 2,200 people in the research and development department and a bunch of quite superb mechanics who are paid as mechanics rather than *racing* mechanics and who regard going to the races as an honour.

In contrast to Ferrari, where I felt I was racing for one individual, the Commendatore, at Porsche I quickly formed the impression that I was driving for the Porsche company name. Ferry Porsche is still very much alive, but there is much more of a corporate identity to the company than one senses at Maranello. Porsche does not revolve round one individual. Peter Schutz was the top dog in the management team throughout my time there and I found him most outgoing and easy to talk to. He wasn't the sort of man who only sat back and listened. He had firm opinions of his own—said what he thought and then got on with it.

In charge of the whole research and development office is Professor Helmut Bott, a man for whom I have the most tremendous admiration because he is involved with every new product that comes out of Porsche, plus every bit of development carried out by anybody on anything. I just don't know how he has the time to focus his thoughts on the racing programme and I almost feel embarrassed about taking up his time when I make an appointment to talk to him about racing matters. He continues to shoulder the most remarkable workload, despite the fact that he was quite seriously ill the year before last. Ultimately, I suppose he is the man to whom I was answerable as a Porsche factory driver and, as you will see later, the one I had a bit of a row with after winning the 1986 World Sports Car Championship.

Also reporting to Professor Bott is Peter Falk, Porsche's Competitions Director. I first got to know him back in 1971 during my time with the 917s. An extremely pleasant, almost unobtrusive, individual, he is calm, methodical and very natural. Not generally the sort to let his hair down, but I have managed to get him really relaxed on a few occasions, sticking a few whiskies down him at Fuji in '86, for example. Under those circumstances he assumes a totally different, extrovert personality, roaring away and smoking like a trooper. But that doesn't happen very often, believe me.

Above *Looking worried with Valentin Schäffer, project manager of Porsche's race engine testing department. It was Valentin who first alerted me to the possibility of a Le Mans drive with Porsche in 1981.*

Right *Porsche competitions manager Peter Falk – a man with a calm temperament, well suited to taking the brunt of my annoyance at Kyalami in 1982 and Fuji four years later.*

Down in the racing division, the key engineer on the car development side is Norbert Singer. He is somebody I have the greatest respect for, even if it has been slightly dulled by the way in which Porsche has tackled what I regard as an ill-judged Indianapolis project for 1988. Norbert will not accept one single accolade for the enormous amount of work he does, a typical Porsche man who believes that the company's achievements should stand on their own without any obvious credit being handed out to any one individual. I mean, he pretty well designed every last nut and bolt on the 956, but is supremely reticent about accepting any credit or praise for his efforts. A truly committed and hard working company man.

That sort of thoroughness was typical of Norbert, typical of Porsche.

Norbert eats, drinks and sleeps Porsche design work and whenever he and I have worked on a project I like to feel that we have really come up with the results. I remember when we tested at Paul Ricard with the 924 Carrera GT, he was absolutely spot-on all the time. I would come in after five laps or so and he would suggest stiffening the anti-roll bar. Then I would go out and do five more laps, come back and tell him it didn't seem to be any better, so he would make another slight adjustment, perhaps only another half an inch, to the bar. We didn't simply abandon that line of thought on the strength of one five-lap run. We would take it, say, two stages further just to make certain that I was sure about that initial impression. That sort of thoroughness was typical of Norbert, typical of Porsche.

In fact, that 1980 pre-Le Mans test sticks in my mind for several reasons. We did a tyre test on the afternoon of the first day and then, at the end of the fourth day, we did some more tyre evaluation work. At one point the tyre technicians said, 'What did you think of that last set?' I replied, 'Funnily enough, they feel rather like the set I used just after Monday lunchtime'. And they replied, 'You're right. We put them back on just to check you out!' They threw that sort of wild card into the equation from time to time, just to keep the drivers on their toes and to check they were not making things up.

Later on, I remember setting out on a 20-lap run and, after only five laps, Norbert stopped hanging out pit boards with my times on. At the end of the stint I asked him why. He replied, 'Well, every lap was pretty well the same, to within a tenth of a second, so there didn't seem a lot of point'. Unconsciously he had put his finger on one particular aspect of Porsche team membership that I love. They never tend to blame the driver. They basically have confidence in the guys they have hired.

Norbert was always prepared to listen. If Ickx and I, for example, were working on a car and you went to him with some technical suggestion, there would be none of this, 'Well, we've done that before and know that it doesn't work'. Quite the opposite, in fact. He would listen carefully and say something like, 'That makes sense', or 'OK, we'll give that a try'. Even on occasions when I said, 'Look, Norbert, I know you are going to tell me you've done it before, but I really would like to try so-and-so on the car,' he would say 'Fine, let's get on with it'.

Back at the factory, Norbert is the sort of guy who gets down to his serious design work when everybody else has gone home. Out at the races, his personality permeated through the entire team. Outstandingly even-tempered, I have never seen him upset. In fact, the whole operation is so disciplined and calm that I have never seen a Porsche mechanic so much as running, let alone heard anyone in the management team raising his voice. No scrambling about, knocking tool boxes off the pit wall in their hurry to get the job done.

Norbert's calm temperament even survived through that terrible fire in the pits at Hockenheim in 1985 when he got quite badly burned. But he was back on the scene again remarkably quickly and it didn't change his personality at all. I just can't praise his contribution sufficiently. To me, he was a crucial lynchpin in the entire operation.

You may now understand why I was reluctant to quit such an ordered environment when approaches were made to me by Jaguar in 1985 to join the Tom Walkinshaw team. With Porsche I had enjoyed such a 'quality' life, with no back-biting, aggravation or recriminations to speak of – well, until 1986, in any event. There was never any of this, 'Well, the driver couldn't drive a sheep to market,' sort of thing. You felt you were all *part* of the operation, I suppose, rather than being an *employee*. I was comfortable there and, as a Porsche driver, I was winning races in America as well, so I certainly didn't relish the idea of kicking off with a whole new project. Starting with Jaguar would have meant two years at least before winning anything significant and that's how things worked out. At that stage of my career I didn't really want to revert to the role of development driver.

I thought the 934 was quite a nasty little car.

After the 917, which was quite simply the fastest and most spectacular machine I had ever driven, my next serious encounter with Porsche was with the Group 4 Porsche 934s and Group 5 935s, both of which had grown out of the development Turbo Carrera. My initiation into this type of car came when Max Moritz asked me to drive his Jaegermeister-backed 3-litre 934 in the 1976 Group 5 Nurburgring 1,000 km race, sharing with Helmet Kelleners and Reinhardt Stenzel. When I got there, he told me that they would also like me to share their Group 4 934 as well, along with the other two and Gunther Steckkonig. I told them I hadn't realized they wanted me, in effect, to drive the whole 1,000 km on my own. All I did was to leap out of one car into the other and wound up absolutely knackered!

To be honest, I thought the 934 was quite a nasty little car. It only had a small wing on the back and quite narrow wheel rims, but still kicked out almost 500 bhp and, with the engine overhanging the rear wheels, it felt quite a spooky proposition. The 934, of course, 'grew up' into the Group 5 935 which was allowed a bigger rear spoiler and wider wheels and I drove one of Georg Loos's cars the following year at Silverstone and the Nurburgring.

'You're a second slower than Klaus Ludwig. What's up?'

I remember coming back into the pits at Silverstone and Loos saying to me, 'You're a second slower than Klaus Ludwig. What's up?' I remember thinking what the hell did that mean, but just answered, 'Well, I've never driven the damn thing before, so I don't think being a second out is too bad!'

After the session I spoke to Ludwig and he asked me what boost pressure I was running. I said, '1.25-bar, just what it started out with'. So he replied, 'Oh, you ought to turn it up higher than that'. I said, 'What will Georg say to that?' and Klaus just grinned, 'Don't worry about Georg, you just turn it up'.

I thought, now that's all very well. These other guys have done well for Loos over quite a long period, but if I blow up one of his engines in my first race, that will be my lot. Then I twigged that all the regular old hands at the game would trickle back into the pits after a quick run with the driver's door slightly open, and their hand out trying to turn back the boost tell-tale indicator!

Anyway, the 935 was a bit less of a handful than the Group 4 car and, by the end of its development, was built round what was essentially a tube-frame chassis rather than purely the production steel bodywork of the original car. It gradually developed better track manners and was always a bit tricky going into a corner with that engine hung out at the back, but it had a lot of sheer grunt and terrific brakes. It really stopped superbly.

The new 956 was a splendid piece of tackle from the very first time we ran it.

Of course, when the Group C endurance programme began at the start of 1982, the new 956 was a splendid piece of tackle from the very first time we ran it. Jacky Ickx, Jochen Mass and I took it to Paul

Good times! Coming up to lap the Nimrod-Aston Martin in the tight 'bus stop' chicane at Spa with my works Rothmans Porsche 956 during the 1982 1,000 km race at the spectacular Belgian circuit.

Ricard for its preliminary tests and, really, it ran incredibly well. We never had any significant testing problems with it at all. Then we took it to Silverstone for its first race and, would you credit it, Porsche suddenly appreciated that they were not fully conversant with the new regulations limiting the amount of fuel you could use.

Prior to the start of the season, I well remember Professor Bott telling me about the forthcoming new car when he offered me my new contract. 'It is the first monocoque car we have built, the first ground-effect car and the first time anybody has tried to fit an air-cooled flat-6 engine into a monocoque. But we have never yet been wrong.' Although I wondered for a few fleeting seconds whether I actually needed all this drama, the fact is that I signed immediately. The 2.6-litre engine had originally been developed for the abandoned Indianapolis project and revived to power the 936 we used to win at Le Mans the previous year. Fuel capacity was restricted to 100 litres under the Group C regulations and we were only permitted five stops during the course of a 1,000 km race.

To cut a long and painful story short, Porsche did not fully appreciate the implications of this fuel restriction and we never got a sniff of the winning Lancia, which was driven by Riccardo Patrese and Michele Alboreto. I shared with Jacky and, towards the end, we were cruising the whole lap in fifth gear, including the chicane, just to make it to the finish. It was an absolute bloody joke from the point of view of the paying public, lapping six seconds slower than we did during qualifying. It was just nonsense and has coloured my opinion against fuel consumption racing from that day to this. I don't believe it has any relevance to motor racing at all. We're involved in the entertainment business and esoteric regulations like that, which the public can't understand, do absolutely nothing for the sport's credibility.

One of the most remarkable aspects of the 956 was that it was virtually spot-on from the point of view of competitiveness right from the outset, aside from the consumption situation. Apart from progressively going stiffer and stiffer on springs, we made very few alterations to the cars' set-up.

At the end of the 1984 season new constructional regulations demanded that the driver's footbox be situated behind the centre line of the front wheels, so the 962 replaced the 956, although essentially it was a very similar racing car. Throughout this period Dunlop did a wonderful job developing suitable tyres, bearing in mind that they had never been involved with ground-effect cars prior to the Porsche 956. I think it's fair to make the point here that I was very critical of them at the time, perhaps feeling that we were not getting the best equipment, but I now know just how much of a job they were doing.

However, the 962 had 19-inch diameter rear wheels, two inches bigger than on the earlier car, and while this helped us to use a slightly bigger ground-effect 'tunnel' under the chassis, I felt the car's handling became rather unstable at high speed, particularly when turning into the corners. Meanwhile, the customer 962s ran on 16-inch wheels all-round, so while we were winning races, people like Bob Wollek and Klaus Ludwig didn't have a clue what we were moaning about. Anyway, although it was a tremendous season, which ended with me becoming the first endurance racing World Champion, sharing the title with my team-mate Hans Stuck, I never thought the 962 ever really developed into a car which was nicer to drive than the 956.

One point that I do want to take up in connection with the 956 is that a lot of people reckoned it was dangerous. 'You don't want to get involved in a big frontal impact with a 956,' was one of the remarks. Firstly, I must say that I've driven many differing Porsches over the years and I have a great deal of respect for their safety considerations. Sure, they could build a carbon fibre composite and honeycomb chassis like the Walkinshaw Jaguar, but one reason they don't is to keep the price down for the private customer because otherwise it would cost an absolute King's ransom.

Certainly the 962 was a safer concept, conforming to the new constructional regulations, but it is extremely important to remember that times and standards change. I think I proved that when I rolled one end-over-end at Sears Point at the end of 1985 and walked away. If you look at things objectively, you could reason that the 917 was an absolute death-trap. Your feet poked out way ahead of the front wheels and, even later than that, I remember some lightweight body panels fitted to one of the Gulf Mirages distorting so much on the Mulsanne straight that I could hardly pull my foot off the throttle pedal and get on to the brakes at the end of it. The body panel had deformed slightly and trapped my toe!

So it's important to remember that priorities change. In 1971 we never dwelt on these considerations to the same extent, but then I suppose a lot of people died in those days and you tend to focus on fatal accidents much more in the 1980s.

I suspect that Stefan would have been killed whatever car he might have been driving.

A lot of attention was drawn to the question of Porsche's structural integrity after Manfred Winkelhock was killed at Mosport Park in 1985 and then Stefan Bellof died at Spa in that enormous accident after he collided with Jacky Ickx. People tend to forget that Manfred slid into an immovable concrete barrier, with no flexibility at all, and Stefan had a massive head-on impact at high speed. I suspect that Stefan would have been killed whatever car he might have been driving.

Although I shared with Ickx at Silverstone and to win Le Mans for my third time, for the remainder of the races in 1982 my co-driver was Vern Schuppan. I find it rather difficult to talk about Vern in this book because he's a friend of mine yet, inevitably, what I have to say about him will be construed as critical.

To say we were jinxed wouldn't even make a start on it.

Don't get me wrong, I think Vern is an excellent driver, probably deserving more success than he has actually achieved. When you look at his racing record, he really hasn't won a great deal, but he's driven very well on occasion. Yet, for some reason, whenever I drove with him it was the kiss of death to my chances. You could positively guarantee that we were going to have a bad time together. To say we were jinxed wouldn't even make a start on it.

I obviously believe I'm quicker than him and, presumably, he must feel that he's quicker. He must do that in order to motivate himself. At Fuji we were well in the lead when the car picked up a puncture, the tyre burst and knocked the suspension off. Then we went off to the Kyalami 9-hours, by which time I was getting rather twitched up about sharing with Vern, and then walked straight into the first of only two major rows I ever had with the Porsche team management.

I arrived there to find that Ickx and Mass had the conventional mechanical fuel injection on their 956, while Vern's and mine was equipped with the Bosch Motronic electronic system which was still at the development stage. So I went out in qualifying and, sure enough, the engine was spluttering and banging its way round, with what felt like three minutes of throttle lag every time you put your foot down.

This was a literal nightmare during practice after dark, because finding the apex of a corner is pretty difficult at night, let alone when the problem is compounded by an engine which has totally unpredictable characteristics. So, after the last night practice session, I went up to Peter Falk and told him the whole thing was a complete joke. I was quite upset and emotional about the whole affair. It just seemed ridiculous.

I knew Jacky was a shrewd old customer when it came to playing this sort of game.

Peter tried to explain to me that every race must be part of the factory race development programme, but I wasn't really in the mood to accept that sort of reasoning. 'OK,' I replied, 'if that's the case, then why hasn't Ickx got it on his car?' Falk laughed rather nervously and said, 'Well, he said he didn't want it.' It was the first time I had heard *that* philosophy spoken aloud!

I knew Jacky was a shrewd old customer when it came to playing this sort of game. If he reckoned any component was likely to give him a performance advantage, he would use it on his car and make sure nobody else had it. But he wasn't one to experiment with unsorted development items.

So the debate continued with me telling Falk that I wasn't happy about getting out in the race with Vern to watch Jochen and Jacky steam off into the distance. I said, 'Look, the people in the grandstand won't be thinking that Bell and Schuppan are running fourth because they've got electronic injection which doesn't work as well as the ordinary system. They'll be thinking what a pair of old tuggers we are for works Porsche drivers!' This sort of experimentation may have been all very well for Porsche, but I certainly didn't see it that way. I said either have it fitted to both cars, or to neither of them.

Poor old Falk eventually agreed to telephone Professor Bott back in Germany and discuss the matter with him. He returned, very sympathetically, to tell me that he would be taking the Motronic off my car. 'Great!' I said. 'Instead, it will go into Ickx's car,' he explained. I must say I found myself thinking, 'I bet after all the fuss I've made, he goes out and wins and we have trouble with the mechanical injection . . .'

During practice we had been bothered by a slight problem on the Motronic-equipped car, to which I didn't pay much attention at the time. Whenever we restarted the engine, flames would come belching out of the exhaust pipe until the engine fired. The evening before the race, I went up to the circuit after dinner to see how the mechanics were getting on and found the Motronic-equipped engine had been installed in Ickx's 956. It was about eleven o'clock at night and when one of the mechanics went to turn over the engine, you've guessed it—in a split second there were flames everywhere, the place was almost alight and everybody was leaping about brandishing extinguishers. There was a quirk in the Motronic system that allowed fuel to collect in the engine, so the moment you fired it up it ignited and blew out of the back in a great tongue of flame. After that they decided Ickx couldn't run that engine and it was removed from his car as well!

During the race, for whatever reason, Vern was a lot slower than me and I drove myself into a ball trying to keep up. I ended up driving for five of the nine hours, but Vern managed to lose a lap to Jochen when he was in the car. It was a very tricky situation and I don't really know why. By the end of the race I was making ground on Jacky, but he was in trouble with a misfire and I would have needed another five laps to have a chance of winning the race.

> By the time I'd spent a year watching Ickx and Mass win most of the races, I was getting pretty neurotic.

Vern and I never won anything together, so when Porsche offered me a choice of driving with him, Wollek or Stefan Bellof in 1983, I opted to partner Stefan. Making that choice effectively pushed Vern out of the factory Porsche team, something which inevitably caused some tension which was a shame because he is a super guy. I must say I felt a bit bad about the situation when he came back into the team at Le Mans the following year in the third car and I was in the number one entry, with Ickx again just for this race. However, he turned up trumps on that occasion and won the race, with Al Holbert and Hurley Haywood, which really pleased me. He needed that success at the time and it proved his quality as a driver. But, for whatever reason, I just was not lucky with him. There's no point in debating it, or trying to get a psychiatrist to work it all out. By the time I'd spent a year watching Ickx and Mass win most of the races, I was getting pretty neurotic about the whole affair. I'd had enough of it all by then!

Of course, it was great to drive with Jacky, but there was always that feeling you were in his shadow. Jochen was to discover this in exactly the same way. No matter how well he drove, Ickx was always perceived as the faster, 'lead' driver. Two years later, in 1984, poor old Jochen found himself doing all the donkey work to win the Mosport Park 1,000 km race after Jacky, daft so-and-so, went out and ran what amounted to a 12-mile marathon the night before the race!

He came back absolutely knackered! He was dehydrated, exhausted and not much use for anything the following day. So Jochen drove the lion's share of the race, performed extremely well as he always does, and won the race. On Monday morning all the newspaper headlines were screaming, 'Great drive by Jacky Ickx', and you had to search through the small print to find out who his co-driver was. That was a classic example of Jacky's star quality rubbing off, irrespective of whom he drove with. I felt sad for Jochen over that and, for the first time, he showed that he was a little bit peeved about it all.

So now I faced the 1983 season with this new boy Stefan Bellof. There was a considerable difference in our ages, he being only 24 and me being 18 years older than him. I used to call him 'my boy' and he referred to me as 'father'. Right from the start it was clear he had the most amazing ability.

Not only was he extremely quick, but nobody used to come back and criticize him for being erratic and unpredictable. In the heyday of Rindt or Rosberg, people came back and said, 'Gosh, you ought to go out to Copse', (or turn three, or wherever) 'he's absolutely unbelievable through there!' I suppose to some extent the fact that we were driving those damn ground-effect cars made him look so controlled, but he was blindingly quick with considerable natural flair. He was an excellent driver with a fine sense of humour, but I didn't want to drive with him at Le Mans, so I was paired with Ickx for that one, which seemed logical in view of our record.

Stefan was blindingly quick, with considerable natural flair.

Of course, Stefan still had that impulsive, youthful enthusiasm which got him into trouble. The classic occasion came in the 1983 Nurburgring 1,000 km. Here he was, a young German, in action at the Nurburgring, running at a million miles an hour, on pole easily, to the point where it was hardly worth me bothering to go out and qualify the car, and then leading the race commandingly after Ickx and Mass had problems.

What happened next was a product of over-exuberance on his part and, in my view, lack of control by the team. When I handed over to him we were about three minutes ahead of our nearest rivals.

Two laps later the pit hangs a board out saying, 'Plus 4 MIN'. So next time round he does a 6 m 35 s lap. Then they put out a board

saying, 'SLOW' and Stefan responds with a 6 m 25 s lap. Next time round he has a massive accident. To me, it was a totally unnecessary accident, a complete joke.

When Stefan got back to the pits, he just laughed it all off. I thought the team would be extremely upset, but they didn't seem to be. Bott, Falk and the others didn't show a flicker of emotion, but I understand that Stefan got something of a once-over when he got back to the factory. If we had won that race I would have taken the World Championship in '83, all other things being equal, so that probably coloured my view of the whole episode!

Ickx won the Drivers' Championship in 1983 and then retired from the cockpit, so I continued with Bellof as my basic co-driver into 1984, although by now I was well involved with Al Holbert racing in North America. The factory team missed Le Mans after falling out with FISA over rule changes, and it was also decided that they would not take works 962s to the sprint races at Brands Hatch and Imola.

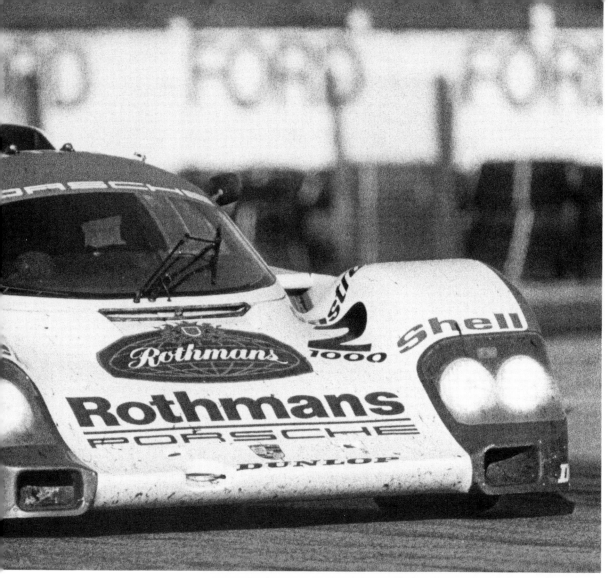

A touch of opposite lock and blazing headlights as I wheel the Porsche 956 through Clubhouse corner on my way to victory in the 1983 Kyalami 1,000 km, sharing with Stefan Bellof. It was my last shot at the World Endurance title that year, but Jacky Ickx took it by three points after finishing the race third with Jochen Mass. **Right** Me putting a brave face on my disappointment as I congratulate the new Champ!

Stefan hitched himself a ride in a private 962 which gave him a leg-up in the points table, enabling him to take the Championship. I was very disappointed about that. None the less, we still had quite a successful year together, winning at Monza, Nurburgring and Sandown Park in Australia.

Stefan left the Porsche factory team in 1985 in order to concentrate more of his time on his F1 programme with Tyrrell, only to be killed in a private Brun Motorsport 962 racing for the lead at Spa against Ickx. I was very fond of Stefan, perhaps identifying in him some of the qualities which I like to think I displayed at the same stage of my own career, and there's no doubt that a great racing future lay ahead of him.

The works Rothmans Porsche 956s come shimmering over the horizon during the 1984 Silverstone 1,000 km race. As well as backing the German team's factory efforts, Rothmans also subtly underpinned endurance racing during a difficult period with discreet assistance, financial and otherwise, in other areas.

There's no halfway house with Hans.

From the start of 1985 my partner in the works Porsche line-up became Hans Stuck, the only other driver I have ever encountered in the same bracket as Ickx as far as being an endurance racer is concerned. He is faster than Jacky, as quick as Bellof, in my view. He deserved far greater opportunities in Formula 1, but never got into the right car at the right time. Terribly competitive, hard and forceful, there's no halfway house with Hans. If he can't drive absolutely balls-to-the-wall, then he doesn't want to know.

'Family photo'! The 1985 Porsche factory line-up. From left to right: Hans Stuck, DB, Jochen Mass and Jacky Ickx.

I admire this incredible, boyish excitement that he still gets from his motor racing. When he comes into the pits it's always at a million miles an hour, adrenalin pumping, eyes flashing—the whole bit. He never seems to have lost that initial wide-eyed enthusiasm and I think that's just great. I have considerable admiration for his skill and ability.

At the same time, Stucky is very gentle on the machinery, believe it or not. He doesn't damage the car and is economical on fuel. Now Al Holbert may say I'm pretty economical when it comes to conserving fuel in his cars, but certainly Hans is more economical than I am. He seems to be able to handle the whole fuel consumption situation better than me and I've never been able to fathom out why.

Obviously, being a German at Porsche, Stuck is top man in the team and he loves it. With Jochen Mass living all over the world as a sort of international citizen, he was never going to be the team's golden boy, but Stucky is. He relishes having everybody running round after him. He does the German national Super Cup series for them, as well as the World Championship, so obviously the whole team has come to pivot round him in much the same way as it centred round Ickx before his retirement.

I suppose I should really have taken the trouble to learn some

Two years later, a title clinched at last. The expressions on the faces of Hans Stuck and myself after clinching the 1985 Endurance Championship at Brands Hatch leave nothing to the imagination. **Right,** *conferring with Stuck strapped in the cockpit. I regard Hans as the only other team-mate I have had who is in the same class as Jacky Ickx.*

conversational German, but it's just one of those things I've put off time and again, aided by the fact that every key person in the operation speaks English fluently. So I ended up thinking, 'Well, why bother?' Of course, that's not the point at all. The real reason why I should have learnt German would have been to relate to the mechanics. In America or, more recently, on the RAC Rally with GM at the end of 1987, it was simply a case of saying, 'OK lads, let's sit down and have a drink'. I can't do that with the Germans, so we inevitably end up having a good laugh about nothing in particular. Because I don't speak the lingo, we just can't share the more personal things which we'd really like to.

Stuck and I shared a factory 962C in 1985, winning the 1,000 km races at Hockenheim, Mosport Park and Brands Hatch, enough to clinch us, jointly, the Drivers' Endurance Championship title. This was the first Championship of *any* sort I had ever won. A *World* Championship. I was elated! Then in 1986, we shared a 962C again, but from the start of the year the Porsche management made it clear that we were going to run the PDK experimental double clutch transmission on our car. This was the first year of the official Sports Car World Championship in Group C, and we never actually managed to win a single 1,000 km race with it all season.

We opened the year with a win at Monza, in a 360 km sprint race, then finished second at Silverstone and at Brands Hatch. The Porsche idea was that we were developing the PDK transmission and, basically, if we won races, then we could regard it as something of a bonus.

As you can imagine, I respected that philosophy for about five minutes. I made the point that Hans and I are racing drivers and we are going out there to win, not just to sit back and be beaten all the time and then get told, 'Oh, it doesn't matter, we're just doing development work.'

As it turned out, the season didn't start too badly and, by the time we had won Le Mans, Stuck and I had amassed 55 points—more than double our closest rivals. But then things began to look a bit rocky. The factory only sent Hans to the Norisring for the Super Cup sprint race there, where I was originally not even intended to race, but we'll come back to that in a page or so. Ironically, this race turned out to be a crucial bonus for me!

I had to chase round to raise the £35,000 sponsorship to hire one of the Joest cars for the race.

An impromptu flag signal from the sponsor at Shah Alam, in Malaysia, during the 1985 Selangor 1,000 km. Stuck and I retired from this race, but by then we had the endurance championship sewn up.

The factory didn't want to race at Brands Hatch, so my business manager David Mills and I had to chase round to raise the necessary £35,000 sponsorship to hire one of the Joest team cars for the race. We had to do it again for the last three races of the '87 season. I don't believe that any World Champion should have to do that. It was a very disappointing state of affairs.

We finished second at Brands Hatch to Bob Wollek and Mauro Baldi, with Derek Warwick fourth in the Jaguar XJR-6, now looking like the strongest challenge to our title efforts. Then, to my disgust, neither Porsche nor Rothmans wanted to go to the Spanish race at Jerez, highlighting one of the big problems of the series, namely that people can drop out when they want to. In that respect, I admire the Formula 1 system whereby you have to commit yourself to a full season in order to score any championship points at all. I suppose the trouble is that there is not a sufficient number of two-seater teams knocking on the door, wanting to participate, to enable such a system to be imposed. It would probably bring the whole sports car racing business tumbling in on itself like a pack of cards.

The next major blow came at Nurburgring where Stuck ran into the back of Mass, totalling both the best works 962Cs, so we wound up going to contest the final race at Fuji, in Japan, with the spare car which not only had PDK transmission, but also ABS anti-lock brakes on it as well. That meant that we were planning to go out and race for the championship with a car which would be 100 kg over the weight limit. It was clear that we would not be competitive.

Hans and I took the matter up with Peter Falk. We had 82 points in the Championship, but Warwick was now well into his stride on 69. Warwick and the Jaguar team had to finish second in order to take the title from us. Third place would do nothing for them. We seemed, on paper, to be in a comfortable position, but there was little doubt that the Jaguar looked a more competitive proposition at this circuit.

Eventually, after some more argy-bargy, it was decided that we would run without the ABS brakes, but the PDK transmission remained. No matter that there are standard gearboxes in the back of the garage, we had to start with the PDK and were made to feel like kids.

Stucky was driving right on the limit to keep in touch with Mauro Baldi's Liqui-Moly Porsche 956B, side-swiping a slower car as he began the lurid business of lapping the also-rans. He went off the road, burst a tyre and came limping in with a damaged undertray. Anyway, that was repaired and we got back to second place, aided by the pace car coming out, and we picked up our rhythm again. Then I came in, handed over to Stucky and, as he let in the clutch—BANG! A drive shaft broke. It took ten minutes to change it, putting us right out of the hunt.

I was absolutely smouldering, brooding about a golden opportunity lost.

I must admit, I was absolutely smouldering, sitting at the back of the pit brooding about a golden opportunity lost. At this point, Brian Kreisky, a freelance cameraman and film maker who covers all the endurance events, comes up to me and opens his interview by saying, 'Derek, what do you think about your chances now?'

I just let off with a great stream of invective, something along the lines of, 'The whole business has been ------- ridiculous. Here's Stuck and I with a chance to win the championship and all we're doing is a bloody development exercise. You'd have thought Porsche would have had more loyalty to their drivers'. And I just ploughed on and on, digging myself deeper and deeper into the mire, as things turned out.

In the end, Warwick and Eddie Cheever were classified second, so that was our title down the drain. However, there was some question as to whether the Jaguar had finished on the same lap as the winning private Porsche 956 driven by Paolo Barilla and Piercarlo Ghinzani. Further detailed scrutiny of the computer timing sheets revealed that Warwick/Cheever were, in fact, a lap behind. They were third. Stuck and I were World Champions!

By this time I was back at my hotel, feeling pretty bruised about it all. Then the telephone rang and it was my business manager, David Mills, phoning from England. 'Congratulations, Sport,' he says, 'you've won.' So I just lost my rag with him. 'Don't be bloody daft, David,' I replied, 'Warwick finished second. We lost.' But he insisted. Eventually I said, 'Look, I'm telling you. We *didn't* win. I'm here only eight miles from the track and you're 8,000 miles away. I know what happened!' Eventually he got the message through to me and I understood. It was just too good to be true!

Then I suddenly stopped in my tracks as a dreadful thought hit me. That interview with Brian Kreisky! I'd been slagging off Porsche for spoiling my chances and now we were World Champions after all. I ran round the place like a maniac trying to find him but, too late, he had gone. That night the whole interview went out by satellite, on one of the sky channels. I couldn't bear to think about the reception I would get when I next visited the Porsche factory.

I tried not to think any more about it. After I got home, I arranged to see Professor Bott a couple of days before the presentation of the Porsche Cup awards in Germany. So he invited me to lunch and I arrived to find a nice little studio room outside his office where the table was laid for two people. Then he arrived, pleasant as ever. 'Good morning Derek. Congratulations on the championship. But there is one thing I would like to speak with you about. I was not very happy about your comments from Fuji on the television . . .'

I remember I was just about to put the soup spoon to my lips and I absolutely froze. I couldn't get a word out. So he went chattering on, reminding me of the Porsche philosophy, of how he had to justify the racing programme to the Board of Directors, how every race has to contribute to the development of a specific component. How could I do anything else but accept what he was saying?

When he finished, I just said, 'Look, I totally understand what you are telling me, but I will never believe that it was the correct decision

Looking thoughtful, waiting for my stint in one of Al Holbert's IMSA Lowenbrau Porsche 962s. My racing programme in North America has become every bit as important to me during the last few years as my World Championship efforts with the Porsche factory.

to run the PDK transmission in that race. I'll make myself available for three weeks of testing at Paul Ricard during the winter if necessary. I'll test anything for as long as you like, but I don't think it was right to experiment at a race where we stood to win the World Championship'. I felt that strongly about it and, for all the trouble my remarks had obviously caused, I like to think that Professor Bott saw my point of view as well.

Returning for a moment to that Norisring race, Stuck could have emerged with the Championship effectively won if he had managed to score points in this home event, a detail which I'm certain had not escaped the Porsche management who would obviously have liked a German World Champion. Although I had the offer of a Kremer team car on Yokohama tyres, I really didn't think I would bother. A few weeks earlier I had driven one of the Brun team cars to third place in a Hockenheim sprint race, running on Michelin rubber, and since I figured the Michelins were not as good as our regular Dunlops, I concluded that the Yokohamas were not going to be much to get excited about. The previous weekend I had finished fourth in the IMSA race at West Palm, Florida, sharing Al Holbert's 962.

Then, out of the blue, John Fitzpatrick phoned me and asked if I would race at the Norisring for him. Initially I thought well, no, I won't bother, but then I remembered his car would be running on Goodyears, in contrast to the Dunlops we used on the works cars, so I agreed. It was a bit embarrassing, having to let Kremer down, because my name was on his car when I got to the German circuit.

Of course, I'd never given a thought to the fact that Fitz's entry was a 2.6-litre 956-engined car, as opposed to the 2.8 and 3-litre 962s and, in the event, the car was diabolical. It was painfully, visibly slow, but I drove my backside off from virtually last place on the grid, struggling round to take 11th place shortly before the end.

I thought, if only I could finish tenth, then I would pick up a single Championship point which would be useful later on. Of course, Stuck should have won by about four light years with the works car, but was delayed with electronic trouble and eventually wound up 15th. So, at the end of the year, I was given the title ahead of Hans on the basis of this tie-decider—11th as opposed to 15th at the Norisring.

My racing programmes in the USA have really taken off in a big way over recent years.

Of course, no account of my experiences with Porsche would be complete without mentioning my racing programmes in the USA, which have really taken off in a big way over recent years. I struck up the acquaintance of Bob Akin and he asked me to drive his 935 at Daytona in 1981. We finished second and repeated this result in 1982. Later I drove a BMW M1 at Watkins Glen with David Cowart and Kenper Miller after Le Mans in the summer of '81.

However, by the summer of 1981, although I'd won Le Mans with Jacky, there wasn't much about for me to race. I had the promise of a Porsche deal for '82, but financially I found myself in a pretty dire situation. I wasn't getting much more in the way of IMSA drives on a regular basis with Akin, so it was difficult for him to keep paying me on a regular basis. Anyway, I fixed up a drive in a highly touted Porsche 934 with a guy called Chatz Vincenze. It was arranged through F. David Stone, the Canadian journalist who used to be press officer for the Mosport circuit, and he told me that the car had finished in the top ten in every race so far, just by tootling around. I bit the bullet, bought the air ticket as cheaply as I could, and flew out there.

It was a really humbling experience, believe me. I've been pretty realistic during my time as a professional racer, but after spells at Ferrari, Renault and Porsche, wallowing about at the back of an IMSA field turned out to be a pretty sick-making experience. This was also a round of the World Endurance Championship, so I was feeling low by the end. We finished so far back, misfiring for most of the race, that it hardly mattered. It was a shocking business.

Then, out of the blue yet again, I got an offer from Porsche 935 privateer Mauricio DeNarvaez to drive at Elkhart Lake the following weekend in the next World Championship round. I qualified reasonably well, but then blew up the engine during the race morning warm-up. There was nothing for it but to fit the engine which had raced to third place at Mosport the previous weekend and, for some reason, it just guzzled fuel like you wouldn't believe. I was in every ten laps or so and wound up 17th. Another big disappointment.

While I was at Elkhart Lake, I was approached by Alvin Springer, one of the most respected Porsche preparation specialists in the USA, and asked whether I would like to share his 935 with Rolf Stommelen in the following weekend's Lumbermans 500 at Mid Ohio. Harald Grohs, who'd co-driven Rolf to victory at both Mosport and Elkhart, wasn't available, so I was being offered the deal.

I replied, 'Yes, that's great', so Alvin asked me how much I wanted. I asked him for $3,000, so he responded by suggesting that I had a share of the prize money. That way, he would not have to pay out if the car retired. Well, I figured there was no way we would beat all the Can-Am cars, so I opted for the flat three grand. Of course, when it came to the race, the Can-Am cars went flying off in all directions and we won! I suppose I kissed goodbye to about $10,000 by not taking up his original suggestion for a share of the prize money. Ever since that, Alvin and I have always laughed about it every time we've met!

I kissed goodbye to about $10,000 by not taking up his original suggestion.

For the next couple of years I rather dabbled with the IMSA series, not taking part in a full programme, until the start of 1984 when a really terrific proposition came my way. During my time with Akin, I had got involved with some promotional work for Camel, the IMSA series sponsor, and got to know very well a PR guy by the name of Tom Tucker. I used to travel with him a lot and here and there he arranged for me to do press and promotional work for the series which all turned out to be quite enjoyable.

At the start of 1984 he phoned up and said he had some backing from Marlboro, who own the Lowenbrau name in the USA, and asked, 'If you had this money available, what would you do with it?' I instantly replied, I'd contact either Al Holbert or Alvin Springer of Andial to run it. So Tucker said, 'Well, would you mind if I made a direct approach to Holbert,' and I said that was fine.

Within an hour, he was back on the phone telling me that he had not only put a deal together with Holbert, but that the engines were going to be prepared by Alvin Springer. I said, 'My God, that's fantastic!' It took some time to get the contract finalized, but eventually we got the third 962 to go to the USA, after Bruce Leven and Bob Akin got theirs.

There was no question of Porsche allowing Holbert to jump the queue, so eventually we had to hire Bruce Leven's 962 to get our show on the road. Of course my partnership with Holbert was immensely important and has been ever since.

Nothing much has really been written about Al Holbert, but I can't say enough about him. He is a very quiet, deeply religious man who runs a remarkably neat, tidy and efficient operation. Outside my time with the factory Porsches, I can honestly say that I've never raced for a better, more efficient organization. Al is straight as a die, totally honest, and we have never had a written contract between us.

Al is straight as a die, and we have never had a written contract between us.

In terms of driving style, he models himself on the examples of Bruce McLaren and Mark Donohue, always trying to perfect little developments to give the team an edge. He just gets into the car, does two laps, comes in and says, 'Right, we'll take a little bit of camber off there, adjust the bump rubbers on the rear shock absorbers, stiffen the springs at the front and drop the ride height half an inch'. I find it all intriguing because he does make his cars absolutely beautiful to drive.

A lot of people say, 'Ah, Holbert's got a better car . . .' But my answer to that is, if he's got a better car, that's because he has *made* it into a better car. As a driver, he is outstanding and very underrated. Look at his record; he's won Le Mans twice, Daytona twice and the IMSA title three times.

I think the best insight into Al Holbert's character could be seen by his actions at the start of the 1985 season, our second with Lowenbrau. I suggested to him that perhaps Lowenbrau should put something into the budget for PR appearances, so we agreed a figure and he went off to make a proposition to them. Well, they accepted—but only for 50 per cent of the figure we had in mind!

Al immediately contacted me and said, 'Derek, good news, bad news . . .' and then went on to recount the outcome. He then said, 'But don't worry, I'll give you 80 per cent of what they are offering'. I thought that was extremely generous, a reflection, I believe, of the contribution I was trying to make to his overall team programme.

Although Al appears outwardly very serious, he has a great sense of humour. But he guards against being too light-hearted in public and, of course, his other recent recruit for the 1987 season, Chip Robinson, is a serious-minded and determined young man who ended up winning the IMSA drivers' title.

'Right, now it's our car, we want our names above Klaus Ludwig's on the side.'

First time out in the Lowenbrau 962 was at Riverside where we lost out by a couple of seconds to Randy Lanier and Bill Whittington in their March-Chevrolet. The Whittington brothers, Don and Bill, were some of the more colourful individuals I was to encounter on the US racing scene, having first come up against them in Europe when they used to turn up and buy cars and drives for cash. I remember they went up to Kremer at Le Mans in 1979, asked how much to buy his 935, went away again and returned the following day with the dollars to pay for it. They said, 'Right, now it's our car, we want our names above Klaus Ludwig's on the side.' Then the three of them went out and won the race!

They had money like you and I cannot believe. At any one time they seemed to have three 935s on hand, with no sponsorship identification at all. They were not brash, in fact they seemed quite unobtrusive people. I was locked into quite a tight battle for the 1984 IMSA title, against Bill Whittington and Lanier in that March, and they always seemed very respectable guys, not the sort to cause any trouble.

One of the most memorable dices I had that year was against Bill Whittington in the March at Watkins Glen. It was real no-holds-barred stuff, which I loved, with no worries about having to back off because of fuel consumption considerations. I started from pole in the Lowenbrau Porsche and we got tangled up in a terrific dice which seemed to go on for hours. That Chevy-engined March was a little quicker out of the corners, but I could pull him back under braking. It was fantastic stuff, but then, around half distance, I tried to dive

With Al Holbert after a victory at Watkins Glen. Holbert is an absolutely straightforward guy, totally reliable and a super test driver with a flair for working out chassis set-ups which are pleasant to drive.

inside him going down that hellishly bumpy back straight at Watkins Glen and—ZAP!—he just cut straight across in front of me!

My instinct told me to take to the grass, but there was a damn great Chevy Corvette parked on precisely the spot I needed as a run-off, so I just anchored up hard, went under the back of the March and waited for the impact. Miraculously, nothing happened. Eventually I overtook him and we went on to win the race.

Bill Whittington retired and, later in the day, came by and said, 'Hey man, that was fantastic—the best dice I've ever had in my life'. So I replied, 'You bloody near killed me. What were you doing?' He looked surprised and asked me what I meant, so I explained that he had just chopped across me without a glance. He became very apologetic. 'I'm sorry . . . the mirrors on that March are pretty bad. I couldn't see a thing . . .' So we both shook hands and I gave him the benefit of the doubt. Sure, it had been a great race, but I made a mental note of what had happened out on the circuit.

Later that year I was driving the 962 in the Daytona finale, by which time Lanier had won the championship ahead of me, with Bill third. I came round the banking in the lead and found Bill's March in the middle of the track. Remembering the episode at the Glen, I figured that it might be better not to pass him on the outside, just in case he eased me into the wall.

Anyway, I opted to come low down and pass beneath him. So as I slipped inside him, lo and behold, he dealt out the same hand as he'd played previously. Just chopped right across me! I literally had to throw my Porsche on to the skirting at the bottom of the banking and

Travel stained. The winning Lowenbrau Porsche 962 makes a routine pit stop in daylight on its way to a hard-won victory in the 1987 Daytona 24-hour epic.

Done it! Punching the air with delight, I acknowledge the chequered flag at Daytona, '87. A surge of adrenalin helped me to overcome severe cramp after my penultimate stint behind the wheel and I was in fine form for the final hour driving the Porsche 962.

went bouncing along in a shower of sparks. I thought 'Jeez . . . what is he doing?'

After the race I was really upset and when one of the journalists at the winner's press conference asked me, 'Was there any particular part of the race which was dangerous for you?' I replied, 'Yes, just here, right in front of the press box!' I added that I was very disappointed by Bill Whittington and that I had already experienced a similar incident with him at Watkins Glen. That was all I said at the time.

Since then, I suppose I saw Bill a couple of times, but we never mentioned it. Later events rather caught up with Don and Bill, who are now no longer actively involved on the racing scene.

I don't believe that anybody ever got rich by being a factory Porsche driver, at least not by contemporary Formula 1 standards. I would say you would be hard pressed to find any professional sports car racer who is earning more than $400,000 a year and that would be taking into account all aspects of their programme—promotional work, personal appearances and so on—not merely their earnings from the cockpit.

Of course, the USA is obviously attractive from this point of view.

The IMSA series is quite lucrative and, indirectly, I am sure the World Sports Car Championship has suffered as a consequence. If you win Le Mans, for example, the car will probably earn £15,000— not much for a race length which equates to almost a season of Grands Prix!

You would be hard pressed to find any professional sports car racer who is earning more than $400,000 a year.

By contrast, every IMSA round has a prize fund of between $25,000 and $40,000. Drivers earn between 25 and 50 per cent of that total, depending on their deal, and there is also income to be generated from additional, incidental awards.

Below *Daytona victory, 1987. The winning driving team looking a little less exhausted than they felt a few hours earlier. From left to right: Al Holbert (clutching 'Camel Pyramid' cheque), DB, Chip Robinson and Al Unser Jnr.*

Right *I experienced mixed
fortunes in the 1987 GP of
Southern California, held
on the Del Mar street circuit. My team-mate Chip
Robinson first crashed his
own 962, then took over
mine and subjected it to the
same fate. Afterwards, he
approached me sheepishly
and asked, 'Do you think Al
will fire me?' I replied,
'Well, let's put it this way,
I've never failed to finish a
sports car race in my entire
career through crashing a
car. You've crashed two this
afternoon, within minutes of
each other!'*

Camel, for example, have initiated what's called the Camel
Pyramid, in which every race win is worth a bonus of $10,000. You
then have the choice of taking the money or leaving it in the kitty,
gambling on winning the next race, in which case you can collect
$20,000. If you take the $10,000 and then win the next race, the
$10,000 isn't available to you as the same team. The money then
becomes $20,000 for the third race which you don't qualify for either,
but somebody else can. A lot of the top teams take their $10,000 and
don't gamble on it, I can tell you that!

When we arrived at Watkins Glen in 1987, for example, there was
something like $50,000 in accumulated bonuses up for grabs, on top
of the $30,000 first prize. Later on, in the Grand Prix of Southern
California on the Del Mar road circuit, Jochen Mass came up trumps
and collected an $85,000 dollar first prize which included the
pyramid!

The promoters also have Kodak involved, putting up the Kodak
Copiers Endurance Championship which awards a magnificent trophy
and $50,000 to the car which has covered the greatest number of
racing miles during the course of the season. Our team has clinched
that for the past two seasons.

There is a lot of incentive—and money—
floating round the racing scene in America.

In addition, there is the Camel Championship money, the IMSA
title winner collecting $100,000 at the end of the season, plus
bonuses from the American Porsche Cup system. There is a lot of
incentive—and money—floating round the racing scene in America.

The IMSA series has a splendid atmosphere about it, with plenty of camaraderie between the teams and a great deal of socializing away from the circuit, which tends to keep everybody together. But I think the biggest thing I enjoy about it all is the media attention. That's quite fantastic by comparison with the relatively low level of interest demonstrated in Europe for the World Sports Car Championship.

I get a lot of exposure in the USA. The media is less inhibited about asking questions and they keep returning to the drivers almost every time they come into the pits and climb out of their cars. I was reminded that the same sort of feeling exists in rallying when I did the 1987 RAC Rally in a Vauxhall Astra. No sooner had I taken my helmet off than there were two television cameras waiting to interview me. Obviously, any driver is going to find that extremely satisfying.

It's the same with the promoters. They are positive and enthusiastic about the races they are promoting, unlike some World Championship organizers who seem almost apologetic that they are putting on a sports car race. Usually it's a case of, 'Sorry that we've not got Formula 1, but it's only a sports car race'. A bit second class, that's the strong implication. By contrast, in the USA they take what I consider to be a more positive view, valuing F1, NASCAR, IMSA and CART on the same level, giving everybody the same amount of attention, within reason. Naturally I like that. When you've been racing for as many years as I have, it's nice to get a bit of personal recognition and at the same time see your chosen sport getting some acknowledgement.

The thing I like about IMSA is getting away from the fuel consumption nonsense.

However, as I've said before, the thing I like about IMSA more than anything is getting away from the fuel consumption nonsense which has been the World Championship's bugbear for the last few years. We can get into a really good dice without worrying about consumption and, if you run a bit short, you can nip into the pits for a top-up. In 1988 that will be our penalty against the Jaguar team which is launching a massive IMSA onslaught, but it's much better than being hypnotized by a fuel computer. The IMSA regulations basically rely on differing weight limits for the various cars to equalize the performance and, although we always moan to some extent about any technical regulations, these ones work well and there is plenty of wheel-to-wheel racing as a result.

The leading light in IMSA is John Bishop and, along with his colleagues, he runs a fine series which has done extremely well over the years. If I have any criticism, it is perhaps that the organizers

When the Porsche factory team pulled out shortly after winning the 1987 Le Mans 24-hour race, I found myself in the humiliating position of being a World Champion who had to scrape sponsorship together in order to go racing! Stucky and I finished fourth in the Brands Hatch 1,000 km a month after our Le Mans triumph in this Porsche 962 rented from the Joest team.

have not quite grasped how much international interest and potential the series has developed. In all honesty, you have to say that IMSA is about as bland and anonymous a series title as you could imagine. What the hell does it mean to the uninitiated? If they called it the 'American Sports Car Championship' everybody would know precisely where they were and it would attract even more attention!

Since starting with the Holbert team Porsches in 1984, I have won a lot of races, as you can see in the racing record at the back of the book. As I mentioned, the first year I finished second in the IMSA points total behind Randy Lanier and, in 1985, second behind Al Holbert, which I suppose you could say was neat and tidy for the team. In '86 I was third behind Holbert and Price Cobb, then dropped to sixth in 1987 in the series won by Chip Robinson. I already plan to be back for more on the IMSA scene, with Al Holbert, in 1988!

The recurrent theme throughout all this racing over the past eight seasons is, of course, Porsche. However, I must say that there were some signs of tension at the start of 1986 when it became absolutely clear that the 962C just was no longer a real contender in a straight fight with the Jaguars. Yes, I know we won Le Mans, which is an event apart, but the fact remains that we never really got on terms with the XJR-8s in the 1,000 km races.

I have to put a lot of this down to Porsche failing to take the Jaguar challenge sufficiently seriously. There seems to have been a distinct corporate lack of foresight as to the Jaguar's competitive potential. We really should have built a new car for 1986, but Porsche now seem to have got terribly involved in the Indy project, so a great deal of time has been spent on that. I find it hard to accept, sometimes,

Above *Strong challenge arrives. Working hard at Jerez in 1986 to keep my 962 ahead of one of the new Jaguar XJR8s which provided us with our first serious rivals for years. Jaguar only won a single race in '86, but returned with a vengeance in '87 to win just about everywhere – except at Le Mans!*

Below *Poor fuel economy and an outdated chassis meant that Stucky and I couldn't live with the Jaguars throughout the 1987 Silverstone 1,000 km race, where we finished third in this works 962, its Rothmans identification replaced by Autoglass and Shell Oils on this occasion.*

because I am a competitive racer and I want the right equipment to have a reasonable chance of success.

The 962C's lack of competitiveness led Stucky to add to the tension after the 1987 Autoglass 1,000 km at Silverstone when he was quoted in the German press as saying part of the reason we didn't win at Silverstone was that Mass, Wollek and myself were too old to get the job done.

I was a bit perturbed about this, feeling that if Hans had got anything on his mind then he ought to come straight out with it. Anyway, Jochen was really upset about it and confronted Stucky, who, in turn, denied it. Jochen pressed home the point, saying, 'The rest of us have all been in this team since 1981 and there's never been any back-biting up until now'. Anyway, I was disappointed but, in truth, I think it was just a reflection that Hans wants to win desperately. There is no way that our not being competitive at Silverstone has to do with anything but the fact that the 962C wasn't sufficiently fuel efficient and is six years out of date. End of story!

I don't want to round off my comments about Porsche without referring to that 1988 Indianapolis project. Firstly, I think it is amazing that the prototype was such an obviously bad car. Secondly, I think that the whole concept of their doing Indy will not benefit their image at all. I firmly believe that the Porsche image is so firmly rooted in sports cars, whether production or racing, that the link with Indy will be hard to sustain from an image point of view. I recently spoke to a British Porsche dealer who, by way of conversation, asked me what the factory racing programme involved in 1988. He was absolutely flabbergasted when I told him how the commitment to Indianapolis had reduced the sports car programme. He told me he didn't understand it and couldn't see for the life of him how a CART racing programme could produce any worthwhile promotional benefits. Clearly the Porsche management has its reasons.

But let me finish this chapter on a positive note. I certainly would not be where I am today without Porsche and everything they have done for me as a company and a racing organization. They gave me a chance at the point where my racing career looked like grinding to a halt. If I am honest with myself, I can never really thank them enough.

Chapter 4

Le Mans: the love/hate affair

F ORMULA 1 was always my goal, so I never really 'looked over the fence' and paid any attention to Le Mans. Circumstances took me to Le Mans, not a route which I consciously chose. When you are embroiled in Formula 1 the whole business is so desperate and intense you have the impression that there is nothing else in the world. The drivers, team owners, journalists, photographers and sponsors are really quite aloof and elitist. You get the impression that everything else is beneath them.

I suppose I was like that, to some extent. The only thing I knew about endurance racing in general and Le Mans in particular was gleaned from following the exploits of people like Stirling Moss at Le Mans on my little portable radio in bed at night while I was away at boarding school. I used to follow it because it wasn't possible to pick up the Grands Prix on the radio, so Le Mans was the race I always used to take an interest in.

However, I had no real interest in racing there during what we might describe as my single-seater phase. Only when I became successful with my own first Formula 2 Brabham did the JW/Gulf GT40 offer come my way, but that never gelled thanks to Ferrari warning me off. My route to Le Mans really began in the spring of 1970 when Jacques Swaters, Ferrari's Belgian importer, invited me to drive his 512M in the Spa 1,000 km race. I shared with Hughes de Fierlant and we finished fourth.

Swaters was a super person with an enormous amount of enthusiasm. After that result at Spa he was hell-bent on a Le Mans entry and my reaction was 'Great, let's go for it. Wonderful stuff!'

Then one day Jacques phoned me up to tell me that Ferrari would like me to join the works team and drive a factory 512M at Le Mans. My response to that was quite straightforward. I said, 'Stuff that,

This is the car I wanted to drive at Le Mans in 1970! Jacques Swaters's Ecurie Francorchamps 512M which, seen here, I had driven to fourth place in that year's Spa 1,000 km, sharing with Hughes de Fierlant. The factory pressured Swaters into releasing me to drive the works car with Peterson.

Jacques. What has Ferrari done for me? Pushed me out of his team, that's all, in September 1969. No, I want to drive your car'. To be honest, I reckoned it was a damned cheek Ferrari kicking me out of his team and then trying to poach me from one of his own privateer operations when he suddenly started noticing my form.

Bruce McLaren had been killed at Goodwood in one of those totally bloody unnecessary testing accidents.

Anyhow, Jacques said, 'Well, you'd better come across and talk to me about it'. So on 2 June, two weeks prior to Le Mans, I went up to London and set off to Brussels for a meeting with him. On the way out to Heathrow from central London I was on the airport bus when I caught sight of some news in an evening paper which just shook me to the core. Bruce McLaren had been killed at Goodwood in one of those totally bloody unnecessary testing accidents that seem to happen now and again. By the time I got out to meet Jacques, I was feeling pretty depressed about everything.

Jacques was extremely understanding, but quite insistent that I should drive for the factory at Le Mans. I began to get a bit agitated about this, saying, 'I really don't see why the hell I should. I want to drive for you. I love the whole atmosphere and ambience in the Ecurie Francorchamps team'. He nodded understandingly, but then went on to point out that Ferrari was putting the pressure on him. Not to put too fine a point on things, the implication was that if Swaters didn't ensure that I drove for the works team at Le Mans, then there just might be the odd touch of trouble when and if Ecurie Francorchamps needed spare parts for its 512M . . .

So I drove the 512M at Le Mans for the factory. It was really the first time that I'd come across Ronnie Peterson at close range. OK, we'd driven together in Formula 2, but I can't pretend that I really knew him up to that point. I suppose that was a typical example of how young drivers behave when they are relatively immature, struggling and on their way up the ladder. Everybody is too busy protecting their own career prospects so they've never got sufficient time really to get to know their colleagues. I don't think it is really antagonism, merely a question of playing your cards close to your chest when you are dealing with a close rival.

The top priority was to make sure that *you* got the drive and not the other bloke.

Making your own way in the racing world is the only thing that motivates a driver at that stage in his career. For a variety of reasons, including the fact that people used to get killed, you tend to keep yourself remote from your colleagues and rivals. The top priority was to make sure that *you* got the drive and not the other bloke. As you mature you discuss things more openly with your fellow drivers, perhaps more so in long-distance sports car racing where your joint fortunes in any one race are dependent on one another's efforts. But in those days I didn't know Ronnie well. It was going to be a few more years before I really got close to him and found out what a lovely bloke he was.

Probably the biggest single surprise about that Ferrari outing was that we didn't get one shred of advice about how we were supposed to run the race. I suppose I'd read so much about team work at Le Mans, how everybody tried to work it all out, get their calculations right and so on that it all came as a bit of a shock.

They gave the front-line car, driven by Jacky Ickx and Peter Schetty, the priority treatment and just left us to sort ourselves out. I came away thinking 'Well, that was a useless sort of affair,' because if there was anybody who really needed that sort of guidance in that sort of situation it was Ronnie and me. Nothing like 'conserve the gearbox, use the brakes more than the gears and keep it down to 7,000 rpm, or whatever'. Just 'Go for it. Drive as you like'.

We got into the third hour and I was coming up to pass Reine Wisell in a Filipinetti Lola approaching White House. As I came through this left-hander, I found Reine in the middle of the road and he obviously wasn't going very fast—by that I mean 140 rather than 180 mph. As I came up to pass him, he began edging in towards the apex on the left, so I had to make a split-second judgement and nipped by him on the inside.

Right and below *With Ronnie Peterson in the pits at Buenos Aires in 1971, the year after we shared this works Ferrari 512M in what was the first Le Mans outing for us both. We were offered no advice, given no team orders and got on with things as best we could. The engine blew up early on Saturday evening.*

It was so tight that I had to get on to the grass between the kerbing and the guard rail to squeeze through and, as I came out of the corner, I looked in my mirror to see all hell letting loose behind me. Clay Regazzoni had tried to go round the outside of the Lola in his Ferrari, lost control, and I saw him skating sideways down the track, nose into the guard rail, with sparks shooting out from the front of the car where it was rubbing down the barrier. I thought, crikey, that looks like one enormous accident, but I carried on round past the pits, off and away.

On that same lap, my engine blew a piston and the car rolled to a halt on the Mulsanne straight. After I climbed out I could see smoke billowing over the trees at the other end of the circuit. I hitched a lift back to the pits on somebody's motor cycle and, when I arrived, the Ferrari management was really concerned, asking me 'Who started the accident? What happened?' When I told them I hadn't really got a clue, they said 'Well, you were involved in it, weren't you?' whereupon I explained that I got through before everybody else got tangled up. Suddenly they realized that, when they had seen all the smoke coming up, they lost interest in who went past the pits in front of them and, of course, on the next lap, I wasn't there!

At a time when lots of people were still getting killed going motor racing, Le Mans was the classic macho bullring sort of place.

So that was my first taste of Le Mans. It was a pretty stark experience, a bit like viewing the world through a black and white filter. In contrast to those wonderfully colourful, sunlit days driving the F1 Ferrari, Le Mans seemed drab and full of foreboding. At a time when lots of people were still getting killed going motor racing, Le Mans was the classic macho bullring sort of place. Nowadays I feel very at home at Le Mans, but in those days it wasn't in the least bit amusing. All those Ferraris and Porsches thundering round, mixing in with I don't know what else, added to the lean, languid looks on the drivers' faces as they waited for their turns at the wheel. It left me with some pretty stark memories, I can assure you.

The whole business felt tremendously competitive and everybody looked pretty apprehensive about the entire affair. You could almost read the expressions on the faces of the serious drivers: 'Christ, we were lucky to pull through last year's race—but here I am doing it all again'. I found myself thinking 'What on earth are they doing it for if they scared themselves so much the previous year?' Everybody looked frightened to death.

When I went back in 1971 I was a member of the JW/Gulf Porsche team with Jo Siffert, sharing one of those long-tailed 917s which I talked about in the Porsche chapter. This race was a real, full-scale Porsche presentation. At previous events there had only been a couple of factory engineers attached to our team, but now there were technicians and engineers in all directions. It looked more like a full-blown Porsche factory programme.

We ran near the front in our 917 until the engine began leaking clouds of smoke when a small dowel in an oil gallery cracked and the lubricant began leaking out. Despite pouring a whole lot of special foam into the engine to seal up the crack it didn't work and so we had to retire after 18 hours.

So those were my first two Le Mans outings, driving two of the classic sports-racing cars of their era, the Ferrari 512 and the Porsche 917. These machines were outlawed by the change in regulations which limited engine capacity to a maximum of 3 litres after the end of 1971, yet by a strange coincidence I was destined to meet up again with a 512M and a 917 much later in my career. In 1977 I drove one of those Ferraris, owned by Robert Horne of the Horne's tailoring family, to set a new UK land speed record of 200.66 mph on the runway at Fairford, while I was back in a 917 for the 1981 British Grand Prix 'SuperSports' race which I won!

Of course, as all motor racing enthusiasts will recall, the Porsche 917 and Ferrari 512 were immortalized in Steve McQueen's epic film *Le Mans* which hit the box offices in 1971. Based round the 1970 race, it may have had a pretty frail story line, but as a memento of the race it was absolutely fantastic, relying as it did on live race coverage mixed in with lots of specially tailored material shot using real racing cars during the months immediately after the race.

Jacques Swaters had been asked to supply his 512M and I was hired to double for one of the actors. Directed by John Sturges, who was responsible for *The Magnificent Seven* and *The Great Escape*, no expense was spared to make the whole production look as realistic as possible. It was a tremendous experience for me because, of course, I got to work in close company with Steve McQueen himself. For the best part of a couple of months, his family and mine shared a lovely little chateau and all got on incredibly well.

I had heard from other people that McQueen was a difficult man to work with, and although he showed signs of this to others he got on tremendously well with all the motor racing people involved in the production. But, ultimately, he was *the* Superstar of the whole business. Every girl and young actor wanted to stand by or be with Steve McQueen, or get a quote out of him, or try to upstage him by doing something better. In that respect it was an interesting insight into show business oneupmanship. Everybody has to believe they are the very best. I can only think it must become extremely wearing!

John Sturges had a hard time directing what was to be a story about the 24-hour race because, in the ultimate analysis, what is there in the bare bones of Le Mans to make it sufficiently interesting as a film? As racing drivers all you are there for is to get into the car, get out of it, change your clothes, have a massage, have something to eat, snatch a bit of kip and then get back into the car again. Not really much of a story-line, but of course that was the basis of the film. In all honesty, I was never quite certain what the story-line was supposed to be!

The project had started out with Sturges working for Steve's Solar Productions company with McQueen himself set to act and direct at the same time, the intention being to make the story as close as it could possibly be to a real 24-hour race. To an outsider it was

With Steve McQueen during the shooting of Le Mans *in the summer immediately following the 1970 race. Enormous fun to work with, McQueen was a man with a keen sense of humour and no mean driver himself.*

amazing to watch this team of different script-writers and consultants all working feverishly on the plot and, three weeks into the filming, they still seemed to be chasing round trying to finalize how the story was going to work.

It had originally been intended that Steve would actually drive in the race, sharing a Porsche with Jackie Stewart. But for some reason or other that never came off, though Jonathan Williams had competed with Herbert Linge in a Porsche 908 fitted with cameras front and rear and, by the finish, they had 22 hours of footage. So when we were out on set we would periodically dive into a caravan, sit down and examine a sequence of the film that had been shot during the real race. Then we had to go out and try and duplicate the whole situation on 'the set', so when we saw two Ferraris, a Porsche and a Lola all going through White House, 50 yards apart, we literally had to go out there and do the same thing!

This proved to be immensely difficult, starting off from various places round the circuit and trying to arrive at the correct point all at the same time, with a similar gap between the cars and all running at a suitable speed. After the first three or four days I think McQueen and Sturges realized I was keen to get rather more deeply involved than simply sitting in a car waiting for somebody to tell me what to do. So I found myself in charge of trying to marshal the cars into the required sequence at the start of the shoots. When you've got more than a dozen people all milling around trying to tell each other what they are supposed to be doing it never quite works out, so I tried to co-ordinate all the other drivers. It was great fun for most of the time, but the hanging around was a bit painful.

The cars were all kept and maintained at a garage down at Arnage, from where they were driven out to the circuit at about 8.30 each morning. The crew would then spend the entire morning setting up the scenes prior to the start of filming at about two o'clock in the afternoon. Of course, there was no way you could nip off somewhere else during the course of the morning, because there was always the worry that shooting might have to start early for some reason, perhaps if the weather changed slightly, and suddenly they might have to leap into action. If the sun came out they would have to move quickly because it had been sunny at the start of that year's race, but then if it became cloudy and overcast they would say 'Right lads, we'd better make it eight o'clock on Sunday morning,' so then there would be a further delay as one of the technicians had to spray the cars with dirt to make it look as though they had been racing for twelve hours. And so it went on. It was a real performance, believe me.

After four or five weeks there was a big shake-up in the actual production organization and John Sturges told us to 'have a long weekend off while we sort it all out'. Directors from CBS came over from the USA and, by the time they went away, the film wasn't solely controlled by Solar Productions any longer. I think what had actually happened was that they needed an additional injection of finance to continue the project and CBS had said, in effect, 'Fine, but if we put in our money, you'll do it our way'. The net result was that John Sturges didn't continue working on the film, which was a real shame. I got on very well indeed with him and, at one point, he told me that he would rather have used some of the drivers as actors in the starring roles, because the actors didn't really have much to say in the story and they had to have professional drivers on hand anyway to stand-in for the actors in the live sequences behind the wheel!

Steve McQueen himself was a really gutsy sort of guy, particularly when he was out there driving the film sequences, in with a bunch of professional drivers. I well recall one sequence where we had to come through the old White House S-bend, which we took at about 160 mph in the race and, of course, we were trying to make the speeds in the film look as realistic as possible. Therefore, we ran as quickly as we could, but the tyres were obviously not being used to the same sustained extent that they were during the race proper and therefore were not developing their optimum temperature.

Even though in those days we were running on grooved intermediate tyres, which didn't really need much warming-up as compared with the slicks we started using a year or so later, they were still not developing sufficient heat. Anyway, we were doing this sequence which involved a run through White House up to the tight Ford chicane immediately before the pits. Jo Siffert and Steve were in Porsche 917s and I was in a Ferrari 512. I was leading, McQueen second and Siffert third.

You've guessed it! We all set off, about three feet apart, and I didn't back off as we came into White House. Neither did Siffert. So poor Steve, trapped between us, had to run flat-out at 160 mph through White House because he had no choice! When we got up to the end of the shot at the Ford chicane Steve was as white as his Nomex face mask. He climbed out trembling, but with a smile on his face, saying 'What the hell were you bastards doing to me out there?' Everybody was laughing hysterically, including Steve, but he waggled his finger at me and told me he'd get even with us all.

One day soon after we both went out on a couple of small Husqvarna trail bikes. Steve was mad about his bikes, as anybody who has seen *The Great Escape* will appreciate, and could really ride superbly well. Anyway, we were leaping about on the sand dunes just before the Le Mans pits, when Steve disappeared over the top of a slope for a few minutes. Then he came back and said, 'Hey, this is OK, you can really gun it up here'. So I took him at his word and hurtled over the brow, took off . . . and looked down to see that I was in mid-air right over the top of a rubbish dump. It seemed like a hundred feet at the time, but it was probably only ten. I came crashing down in the middle of this garbage tip and Steve just stood there on the top of this hillock shaking with laughter. He had paid me back good and proper.

The family was with me throughout the filming of Le Mans *in the summer of 1970. Here Pam relaxes with Justin (with Smarties) and Melanie, close by my much-loved Ferrari 275GTB/4 which I later changed for a Daytona.*

Motor cycling with my son Justin and my close friend, the late-lamented David Purley, in 1983. David was long retired from motor racing when, two summers later, he crashed his aerobatic plane into the sea just off the beach near our home. I was there that weekend and rushed down to the shore to see if anything could be done. His death removed a remarkable, devil-may-care personality from our local scene.

Peace and tranquility. On the lawn at Little Welbourne, our home at Pagham, with Justin, Melanie and Pam. We all adore the house, which I hankered after for many years before we bought it in 1981.

Lost in thought while relaxing at home.

With Melanie at Hockenheim, 1985.

With Pam; a rare moment of solitude together!

Right *It seemed only appropriate that I should compete in the last-ever Formula 2 race, at Brands Hatch in 1984. I drove this March and raised some money for that very worthy cause, Racing for Britain.*

Below *Off to work we go! Hans Stuck, Al Holbert and myself on parade at Le Mans in 1986, prior to our first victory together. It was to be my fourth win in the French classic, heading a Rothmans Porsche 1-2-3 grand slam.*

Getting on with it at Le Mans in the works Porsche 962C, on the way to my fifth victory in the 1987 event.

Not so happy! The Rothmans Porsche 962C which I shared with Hans Stuck in the 1986 Fuji 1,000 km. I was seething when I was told that we would have to run the PDK transmission in this race, where the World Championship hung in the balance. When Stucky broke a drive shaft accelerating out of the pits I was not best pleased, as you can see in the photograph on the right. Shortly afterwards, I put my foot in it good and proper, tearing Porsche apart in a television interview – only to hear, much later, that I had won the Championship after all!

Above *My office! Bell's eye view of Silverstone's Copse corner, from the cockpit of my Rothmans Porsche, and me busy earning a living.*

Right *I love my racing programme in America with Al Holbert's team and the IMSA Lowenbrau Porsche programme. Here I am handing over to Chip Robinson at a night pit stop during our run to victory in the 1987 Daytona 24-hours, a race which I believe to be more exhausting and taxing than Le Mans.*

Above *It's getting to be a habit! On the rostrum at Le Mans in 1987 with Stucky and Al Holbert.*

Right *A change of scene. Out on the 1987 RAC Rally with the Group A Vauxhall Astra GTE, and Mike Nicholson in the hot seat! A great experience and one which I hope to repeat again in future years.*

There was another memorable episode which involved filming on the White House section of the circuit. They put a camera on the left-hand verge on the exit of the long left-hander, where we were tending to drift out to the right, over a patch of the grassy run-off area which had been used so much in previous years that the circuit's owners had eventually taken the decision to tarmac it over. Of course, that just tempted us to slide even wider, on to that new section, which in effect meant that the central white line on the road was much further to the left of our cars as we came out of the corner.

Anyway, we didn't notice this camera was there and, after our first run, were asked to do it again. This was another sequence with me leading Siffert and we came through absolutely balls-out, because it was all great fun and we weren't about to get much satisfaction from doing it at seven-tenths because it wouldn't have looked anywhere near so effective or realistic.

On the white line, in the centre of the track, was not only a camera but a body lying behind it!

So we both came charging through White House, Siffert right on my gearbox, and as I eased out to the right of the road on the exit, I saw something which made me do a 'double take'. On the white line, in the centre of the track, was not only a camera but a body lying behind it!

Jo had been all over me through the corner in the 917, that Porsche being a better proposition than the Ferrari, so he almost shaved this lunatic lying in the middle of the track. When we finished the run, Sturges told us the whole sequence looked absolutely great from where he was watching, but I was pretty indignant. I said, 'There's some ------- nutcase lying on the ground in the middle of the corner out there'. So Sturges immediately called up on his radio and said, 'Steve, get back up here quickly'.

I'll never forget the sight as McQueen came roaring up on the bike, hair flowing in the wind, and Sturges said, 'Steve, who the bloody hell did you put in the middle of the road with that camera?' So Steve just grinned and said, 'Oh, it was me!' Bold as brass, lying in the middle of the circuit in order to get a better shot as we both went by at 160 mph within a couple of feet of his nose. Just unbelievable. It's something I'll never forget for the rest of my life.

I suppose one of the great ironies about *Le Mans* is that during the course of the shooting I was involved in the worst accident of my entire career, when the Ferrari just erupted in flames around me and the corner of my face was quite badly burned. Steve and I were shooting a sequence in which we could go thrashing past the camera car—a Ford GT40 with its roof cut off—and that would pick us up as we went by. We were running at about 130 mph and the camera car at around 80 mph, so it looked quite impressive.

We had just completed a run up to the Ford chicane from Mulsanne, when I suddenly became aware that the clutch had packed up. When I came to change down it was just a case of 'crunch, crunch'. Anyway, I turned the car round and chased back after Steve down the track towards our starting point for another run. He'd vanished like a dose of salts in the 917 and I was taking it easy, changing gear without the clutch, until I arrived at Indianapolis corner which, of course, was a right-hander approached from what was really the wrong direction.

Just as I came out of the corner there was this 'pop' and the car erupted into flames. In a split second the whole thing was on fire and, as I was wearing an open-face helmet with a Nomex face mask, you can imagine I thought 'Oh my God . . .' as the fire just seemed to shoot straight up at me.

Immediately I applied the brakes, but it's just amazing how long it takes a car to knock off speed when you're really in something of a panic. I thought it was *never* going to stop. I undid the belts and tried to unfasten the door, but on the 512M there was a clip on top of the door as well as a handle, so you had to turn this clip down and then lift the handle.

Anyway, eventually I stopped the car, managed to leap out and then began running up and down the road shouting for a fire truck. Of course, there was nobody in sight and the Ferrari just burnt itself out at the side of the road. The Ford camera car came by, but wouldn't stop, perhaps thinking it was better to drive on and get help, by which time I had run about 50 yards from the car. Suddenly, as the air got to me, my face began to feel really sore. All I could do was to stand there waiting for the ambulance to arrive, by which time the Ferrari was well and truly ablaze. It was completely gutted, although I understand it was subsequently rebuilt.

So this old blue Renault ambulance turned up, one of those things that looks a bit like a dustbin on wheels, together with Sister Bridget, a Roman Catholic sister who was actually used quite a bit on the film set. The doors were opened up and I was told to get in the back, get my overalls off and prepare for some sort of a precautionary injection.

So I lay down on this stretcher and Sister Bridget tapped on the partition and said, 'On driver'—or something like that—at which point the guy at the wheel let in the clutch with such a jerk that my stretcher burst open the doors and shot out on to the track. Now nobody would believe me if I said that, when he hit the brakes, I went shooting back inside again, but that's pretty well what happened. It was just like a scene from a classic French farce, but eventually they got me secured inside the ambulance and carted off to hospital.

Once I arrived, a doctor came over, looked at me and put some cream on the burns and then, in best French tradition, everybody seemed to disappear because it was lunchtime. So I lay there for a

The worst accident of my career thus far came behind the wheel of a Ferrari 512M which caught fire during the filming of Le Mans. *But this outing, on the runway at Fairford aerodrome, had a happier outcome in 1977. Driving the 512M owned by Robert Horne, I established a new British speed record of just over 200 mph. This outing was arranged by my friend David Mills who, in 1983, was to help me negotiate a release from what was proving to be a rather unproductive contract with Mark McCormack's organization. Since then David has assisted with my business management and acted as my publicist.*

couple of hours before anybody came back, thinking to myself, 'Well, how bad are these burns?' Meanwhile, back at the track, nobody knew which hospital I had been taken to and poor Pam was left stranded with Justin and Melanie, not really knowing what was going on. Fortunately, Steve was a tower of strength and reassured her that I wasn't badly hurt.

I lay there for a couple of hours thinking to myself, 'Well, how bad are these burns?'

So that was about it. They patched me up and I went off to Enna, in Sicily, that weekend to race the Formula 2 Brabham BT30 in the next round of the European Championship. That turned out to be absolute agony because there is a lot of volcanic dust in that area and, no matter how tightly you try sealing up the vizor on your helmet, it seems to percolate everywhere.

It was absolute hell. My skin was all puffed up and its recovery prospects were not exactly being speeded up by pulling a helmet and balaclava on and off three times a day, or whatever. It was also extremely hot, so I was sweating a great deal, which also served to aggravate the wound. Worst of all, this volcanic dust got into the wound, so every evening when I returned to my room I had to take

tissues and try cleaning all the dust out of the scars round my eyes and forehead. Then, of course, I just had to go through the whole nauseous routine again the following day. In the race, my personal discomfort was compounded by an oil leak which sent red-hot lubricant down my back.

Immediately after the Enna race I flew straight back to Paris to consult a burns specialist and was thankful that no damage had been done to my left eye. In that respect, I was extremely fortunate and can only think I must have screwed my eyes closed in a reflex reaction the moment the car caught fire. I still bear the scars, ever so slightly, to this day, but they only really show up when I'm very tired or a bit below par.

That accident marked the end of my involvement with the McQueen film, but I regard it as one of the most interesting and important spin-offs produced by my racing career. Later I went to visit him in Hollywood, about a couple of years after the filming, during which period I think he'd had a pretty lean time because he'd lost a bundle on *Le Mans*. He took me out to dinner with his new wife, Ali McGraw, and I remember she looked absolutely stunning in a casual off-the-shoulder dress which sticks vividly in my mind to this day.

In the years that followed we drifted out of contact and suddenly, one day in 1980, I went into the office at Church Farm and our receptionist said, 'Oh, Steve McQueen just phoned and said he wanted to have a chat with you'. I asked whether he had left a phone number, but he hadn't, though he said he would probably call again. Mistakenly, I thought I had Solar Productions' number, but I had lost it. If I'd known then what I know now, I would have gone out of my way to phone him back. You see, I didn't know he was fighting cancer and, of course, he died four months later. I guess he was just ringing up to tell me and, I suppose, say farewell, I just don't know.

Steve McQueen always used to say, 'You know, I'm not an actor. I just play myself'.

I felt absolutely awful about that. I mean, he didn't suddenly phone me up after seven or eight years without a good reason. It was all very sad. He was an enthusiast who loved his cars and motorcycles and always used to say, 'You know, I'm not an actor. I just play myself'.

After all that, the real Le Mans seemed a little on the dull side when I went back for the 1971 race! By now I was driving the JW Gulf Porsche in the major endurance events and then switched to the Ford-engined Mirages for 1972 when we were very much the also-rans, and Le Mans was handed to the French Matra team without a fight when Ferrari pulled out, having already clinched the

World Sports Car title. Ferrari clearly didn't feel as though they could produce engines which would last a full 24 hours, so rather than risk blemishing their unbeaten reputation they decided to pull out. So, with Matra running at Le Mans and nowhere else, there was never a direct confrontation between the two leading sports car teams.

The Gulf team also decided to give it a miss, so I was recruited by my old mate Jacques Swaters to drive in the Group 4 class in his Ferrari 365GTB/4 Daytona, the last of the classic front-engined V12s from Maranello, sharing with Teddy Pilette and Richard Bond. I was beginning to enjoy racing at Le Mans at this stage of my career and there were several Daytonas contesting this class, including a works-supported entry plus cars from the Scuderia Filipinetti and Charles Pozzi, the French Ferrari importer from Paris.

It was rather a nondescript race for us, as I recall, and we were lying inside the top ten towards the end of the race, fourth in class, when a delightful Ferrari engineer collared me in the pits, pushed me against some tyres and beamed, 'You can get third in your class ahead of Mike Parkes, if you pull your finger out when you get into the car!'

Up to this point our Daytona had been handling like a pig, but it was starting to rain in the closing stages and I decided to have a big go for it. Jacques was a little bit on the cautious side, figuring it would be better to finish the race rather than not finish at all, which was fair enough bearing in mind that it was his car, and he came up to me saying, 'Derek, I would really rather you took things easily and didn't push too hard'. So I think I said something like 'OK, well let's see how things go and whether we can make any ground or not . . .'

I got out there and in fact hauled right up on to Parkes's tail on that very last lap. Going down the Mulsanne straight I figured I could slipstream past him and outbrake him into the tight corner at the end, even though my car seemed to be wallowing all over the place. I thought I had it all worked out, timed to perfection, but as I lined up to get into the right place a slower car got in my way going through the kink and I had to back off. That was the end of it. In a split-second, I'd lost 150 yards!

After the race the Belgian Ferrari was checked over and the mechanics found that the rear anti-roll bar had been broken for much of the race, which explained why it had been such a handful and rolling all over the place like a bag of sand. We wound up fourth in class behind three other Daytonas at the end.

By coincidence, I was using a Ferrari Daytona as my road car at the time, replacing the much-loved silver 275GTB/4 which I had imported from Italy when I was a member of the Ferrari works team. Of course, the Daytona was a magnificent road car and, shortly after the end of the race, Pam and I set off back to our hotel. After a while, Pam said to me, quite quietly, 'I think you're going a little too quickly, Derek,' so I looked down at the speedometer and it was showing 160 mph. I was in the same driving position as I had been in during the race, using the same gearbox, and was still wound up to a competitive pitch. My adrenalin was obviously still pumping and I had hardly noticed the switch from race to road car!

In 1973 Ferrari and Matra confronted each other in a head-to-head battle for sports car honours throughout the season and, as usual, we were consigned to the role of also-rans. That Len Bailey-designed Gulf MR6 chassis wasn't too bad and we were getting 450 bhp from our Cosworth V8s, as compared with the 465 and 480 bhp which were claimed, respectively, by the Ferrari and Matra engine departments. But our car was about 200 lb overweight, which is one of the reasons we could never get on terms.

My Le Mans outing that year turned out to be a fiasco with Howden Ganley and I sharing the car, but retiring quite early on. The sole surviving Gulf soldiered on into the middle of the night when dear old Vern Schuppan rolled it at Tertre Rouge and was briefly trapped underneath. He wasn't the luckiest of drivers even then, nor the most popular when he arrived back in the pits to explain to John Wyer and John Horsman what had happened.

Matra had the field virtually to itself in 1974 because Ferrari pulled out to concentrate on Formula 1, but our Gulf GR7s were still no match for the French cars. At Le Mans I shared with dear old Mike Hailwood and, in about the second or third hour, I handed it over to him and said, 'For heaven's sake, Mike, take it easy. There's this most awful noise coming from the gearbox . . .' So he looked me straight in the face and said, 'Oh well, let's get it over with quickly so we can all get back for a few glasses of wine!'

Well, Mike may have done his best, but the trouble was that the car actually managed to survive. It was leaking a lot of grease from its

Handing over Gulf Mirage GR7 to Mike Hailwood during our run to fourth place at Le Mans in 1974. Early in the race, when the gearbox began making the most ominous grating sound, Mike quipped, 'Let's get it over with and push off for a glass of wine!'

drive shaft constant-velocity joints, but we staggered on and finished fourth. Matras took first and third places, sandwiching the Porsche Carrera RSR of Gijs van Lennep and Herbie Mueller, a portent for the future because that was the car that grew into the wretched silhouette 934 and 935. Our Gulf seemed to be making ominous noises from its transmission right through to the finish, but lasted the distance, which certainly surprised me.

Then, of course, came 1975 and my first Le Mans victory. The team cut back its programme virtually to nothing because of Gulf Oil sensitivity over a US Senate enquiry into allegations that various American oil companies were offering under-the-table financial incentives to certain South American countries to import their oil and their oil alone. There was even some reluctance for them to field a team for Le Mans. As I've mentioned elsewhere, I signed to drive all the other races for Willi Kauhsen's Alfa Romeo team, but ran for the third straight year for John Wyer at Le Mans. Following the fuel crisis, the Le Mans organizers took the initiative in trying to promote a fuel-consumption formula, obliging us all to run a minimum of 20 laps between refuelling stops as well as restricting the size of the fuel tanks. That meant that our cars had to return more than 7 mpg in order to qualify.

I've made my opinions clear on the subject of fuel consumption races elsewhere in this book, so I won't refer to it again here. For me, the most interesting challenge was to be paired with Jacky Ickx in the team's number-one car. Jacky had written to John Wyer asking if he could join the team at Le Mans – and specifically asked if he could share with me. I was very flattered that he should make such a request. Although he had already won Le Mans for John Wyer once before, with a Ford GT40 in 1969, he said it was fair that I should start and finish the race because I was the one who had done all the development on the car.

The Gulf GR8 wasn't a bad car, but we ran specially detuned engines for this event which we revved only to 7,500 rpm rather than the usual 9,500 rpm, because during endurance tests we had discovered that there was a critical point at around 9,000 rpm which would cause the engines to break after three hours' running. They eventually got on top of this problem, but we had to take things easy for this race.

Vern Schuppan was sharing the other Gulf entry with Jean-Pierre Jaussaud and they led during the opening stages, but they were delayed with some electrical troubles on Saturday evening and Jacky and I led from then on. On Sunday morning we thought we were in big trouble when this awful graunching noise started every time you went round a right-hand corner. Jacky brought the car in to allow the mechanics to check it over, but they simply couldn't see anything anywhere. It was just a mystery.

All through the day we grappled with this problem. There are a lot of right-handers at Le Mans and eventually the whole car began to

Above and opposite *The Gulf GR8 only turned out in 1975 for Le Mans where Ickx and I had a nerve-racking run to victory hampered, as it later turned out, by a broken suspension bracket. I was allowed the privilege of taking the chequered flag, but Jacky didn't stint the champagne when it came to the victory celebrations!*

shake and vibrate. We were both very worried, but despite having the car checked over in minute detail each time we stopped there seemed nothing obviously broken.

Finally, with about three hours left to run, we had a long stop to change a cracked exhaust manifold. As you can imagine, this was not the work of a moment. The engine and exhaust were pretty hot by this stage and the bolts were extremely difficult to slacken off, having been well cooked for the best part of 22 hours. Eventually the job was finished, but when I got back into the cockpit the vibration was now a loud thumping noise and the second-placed Ligier of Jean-Louis Lafosse and Guy Chasseuil was making up ground all the time. The French crowd is, of course, tremendously partisan and was shrieking its support for the French car each time round, but we held on to win by a lap. It was a hugely emotional moment for me as it represented the first truly major success I had achieved since the Porsche 917 days, apart from my 1974 victory in the Spa 1,000 km, also in one of the Gulf cars.

When our winning car was stripped down back at the factory the mechanics got to the bottom of that awful noise. It turned out that one of the rear suspension pick-up points on the gearbox casing had fractured, but of course when the car was stationary it was held in the correct position and a quick look round didn't show that it was fractured. When the car moved, so the suspension started to flex and

the car began to steer with one of its rear wheels.

In 1976 Gulf withdrew its sponsorship, so wealthy American enthusiast Harley Cluxton acquired the cars and fielded them under his Grand Touring Cars banner with John Wyer and John Horsman still running the show. I was paired with Vern and we finished a distant fifth after losing a lot of time when first the alternator, then the fuel pump had to be replaced in addition to encountering a lot of niggling minor problems.

We'll come back to the subject of Harley later in this chapter, because I drove for him again in 1979 in one of the Mirages which, in the meantime, had been converted to take Renault engines for the 1977 race as the French manufacturer's second-string team in this crucially significant race. But in 1977 I declined an overture from Porsche and took the decision to join the factory Renault line-up.

Clutch slip at 190 mph? No way! I'd just driven across a frozen stream of water which had been running across the track.

Renault just had to win Le Mans and didn't stint over its efforts. Gerard Larrousse, their team manager at the time, got in contact with me and asked if I would join the team for the 1977 Le Mans effort. We went endurance testing at Paul Ricard in January, February and March, an awful chore, with lots of snow and rain during the night. On one occasion I was hurtling down the long Mistrale straight during one of the night sessions when suddenly the engine picked up revs in top gear at 190 mph. Clutch slip? No way! I'd just driven across a frozen stream of water which had been running across the track. The 'clutch slip' had been wheel spin. Bloody hell! At that point Larrousse decided that we would stop the test and restart the next morning!

I was welcomed into the team as a Le Mans winner. Larrousse offered me a good fee for my services. They were really single-minded about winning that race and absolutely determined to run a 24-hour test at Paul Ricard without any problem. Four of us, Jean-Pierre Jabouille, Jean-Pierre Jaussaud, Patrick Depailler and myself, did four-hour stints in an effort to prove that the A442 could run the distance without trouble. The team was scrupulously fair and very self-critical. If they got to 16 hours and hit trouble, they didn't say, 'Ah, only eight hours to go,' and continue for the balance of the distance once they had repaired it. Oh no, it was back to square one. The clock would start running again and off we would all go, trying for a 24-hour trouble-free run.

It was a delightful little car to drive, but the whole testing business became pretty boring and, interestingly, prior to the 1977 race we never ran through 24 hours without a hitch. But I consoled myself

I got a great kick out of being the only non-French member of the Alpine-Renault team during their Le Mans onslaughts in 1977 and '78. Here I am cornering at Mulsanne in the former event, in which Jean-Pierre Jabouille and I led for much of the way before the engine broke.

Right In deep discussion with the Renault personnel about the car's progress during testing. They were a highly ambitious and motivated group of enthusiastic engineers and, although I wasn't in the winning car, thoroughly deserved their 1978 Le Mans victory.

with the fact that we tried to drive those tests as close to the limit as we could, obviously not what we would set out to do at Le Mans unless the pressure was really on from the opposition.

So off we went to the race. Jabouille planted our car on pole and we led for the best part of 17 hours, building up a three-lap lead by the early hours of Sunday morning. We were just stroking it along, backing off early. But the team had never done Le Mans before and I always suspected that any car that was new to the race, and didn't have a proven reliability record, was going to succumb to engine trouble after constant exposure to long throttle openings on the Mulsanne straight.

Lo and behold, I was sitting having breakfast in the Renault hospitality area, watching the race on closed-circuit television, when suddenly I saw my car coming up the pit lane with smoke pouring out of the back, so that was the end of that. All through the race up to that point we'd been deluged with journalists saying, 'You're going to win, you're going to win!' But I just felt that there was no way we were going to do it.

The Renault management responded to this failure in very positive fashion. 'Right,' they said, 'next year we're coming back to do it properly.' I was asked to be in the team for a second year, which was great, and throughout the autumn we tested at Paul Ricard and eventually managed to get through an 18-hour stint without any trouble.

Having done that, Renault flew one of the cars to the TRC Research Centre in Michigan, the idea being to run the remaining six hours at high speed and this was the only track we could do it at. It is an eight-mile oval, with a couple of 2½-mile straights joined by two 1½-mile bankings. Normally the track is used to test tanks, trucks and road cars, but since we were there during the Thanksgiving holiday most of the country was off tucking into its turkey and plum pudding.

Out of interest the local sheriff turned up to watch, equipped with a Vascar gun. At the time those guns hadn't reached England and we were intrigued by the way in which you could point it at the car and get an instant speed read-out. So there was Jabouille hurtling round this super test track with all of us hoping that he would be pulling about 215 mph coming off the banking when the sheriff points the gun at the car and says, 'Oh yes, that's 125 mph!' We all rather shuffled our feet and said, 'Well, let's hope not'. And the guy says, 'Oh yes, it says here . . . 125 mph'. Well, we told him it ought to be rather more than that. So he picks up his gun again and says, 'This lap it's 130 mph'.

We tried to explain to him, well, er . . . no, we were in fact doing about 212 mph, but he just couldn't take it aboard. As far as he was concerned, his Vascar gun couldn't let him down. The sheer look of incredulity on his face was something to behold. He simply could not understand the fact that perhaps his Vascar gun was a bit beyond those sort of speeds. We tested for six hours, after which the snow came on the scene and we had to quit.

When it came to the race, I shared with Jean-Pierre Jarier and we retired just after two o'clock on Sunday morning with a failed crown-wheel and pinion. But Renault achieved its aim and won the race, thanks to the efforts of Didier Pironi and Jean-Pierre Jaussaud, after which the team withdrew from endurance racing in order to concentrate on the turbocharged Grand Prix project. It certainly had been a tremendously invigorating experience driving for such a youthful and highly motivated team, but once they had withdrawn my racing future looked distinctly bleak. There was not a great deal left, or so it appeared to me.

The 1979 season was probably one of my worst so far.

The 1979 season was probably one of my worst so far, and I was obliged to drive such also-rans as that lumbering Aston Martin in the Silverstone endurance event, but I did get the chance to share Harley Cluxton's Mirage, now running with a Ford Cosworth DFV again after two years fitted with a Renault engine. Harley was, and still is, a great personality and enthusiast who loves coming to Europe to race. I admire him enormously for his youthful enthusiasm and the very European sense of humour he has managed to cultivate over the years. You don't often meet too many Americans with such a keen sense of fun.

I liked driving for Harley a great deal and, of course, he wanted to get involved in more ambitious projects as the years went on. He had ideas that perhaps we could get together on a Can-Am programme and so on, but there was never really the sponsorship and backing to get the whole thing off the ground. He also had some idea that we might put together an Indy project, and although I would dearly have loved to try it, we could never get the sponsorship together. That was a real shame, because I have done just about every international racing category apart from Indy car racing and it would have been satisfying to add that to my racing record.

Vern and I were paired together again for Le Mans and, once more, our lousy luck came to the surface. As the race progressed the engine gradually lost compression and, by Sunday afternoon, the wretched thing was hardly able to haul itself up the pit lane.

Into the last hour it was really crawling along and when I took over again after the final fuel halt firstly the car wouldn't start and, secondly, it just didn't have the urge to haul itself up the slight gradient towards the exit from the pit lane. The mechanics took off the airbox and sprayed methanol into the cylinders to fire it up briefly, but by the time they'd re-fitted the airbox, it stalled again.

The tension was really building up, it being close to the end of the race, and all the television cameras on the start/finish straight seemed to be trained in on us struggling to get our car moving again. Eventually I moved it forward about the length of a pit before the engine stalled and, of course, they pushed me back again, something which you are not really supposed to do at Le Mans. Suddenly, out came this official and said 'finis', waving his hands to indicate that we were being disqualified.

I sat there with tears almost running down my face. After 23 hours and 40 minutes, the thing wouldn't stagger round the last lap.

By this time Jean-Pierre Jaussaud, one of the other team drivers, was pretty keyed up about the whole affair. He walked up to this guy and said, 'Up there are about 45,000 people watching from the public enclosures'. Then he pointed to the television cameras and said, 'Out there are probably another ten million people watching'. Then he focussed on the official and delivered the final line: 'And you are about to become the most unpopular man in the whole of France?' With that, the guy just turned and fled!

Anyway, we managed to stagger away, but I could not coax that car beyond the end of the pit lane. That slight uphill section was just too much for the engine. I sat there with tears almost running down my face. After 23 hours and 40 minutes, the thing wouldn't stagger round the last lap. We were eventually classified 14th.

The following year came the offer to drive the Porsche 924 Carrera GT. I was originally planning to drive a private Porsche 935 but Porsche GB's Press Officer Mike Cotton tipped me off that there would be these three works 924 entries and it seemed like a good idea to get involved once more with a factory effort rather than running for a privateer yet again.

The plan was that I should team with Andy Rouse in the car backed by the English importer. However, just before qualifying Peter Gregg got involved in a road accident on his way to the circuit, the after-effects of which some people don't believe he recovered from right through until the day he later committed suicide.

Gregg was an unusual sort of a bloke, to put it mildly, and was generally perceived as a bit too good to be true back home in the USA. However, he was pretty popular with most of the European drivers because I don't think he tried to project this 'Peter Perfect' image when he was racing on this side of the Atlantic. Anyway, the doctors examined him, said he was suffering quite badly from concussion, and advised him not to drive. Consequently, I moved over into the 'American' entry and shared with Al Holbert for the first time.

Pit stop in 1980 for the 924 Carrera GT driven by Tony Dron and Andy Rouse. I was originally down to share this car, but Peter Gregg's accident resulted in me being moved to drive a sister car with Al Holbert, thereby starting a relationship which has lasted and prospered to this day.

The only matter of any consequence in that race was our climb through the field into the top six by Sunday morning, then a gradual drop back to 13th after suffering a blown piston. I well recall it was wet at the start, and hammering down the Mulsanne straight amidst all that spray the only way I could keep the car going in the right direction was by watching the tops of the trees on either side of the circuit and trying to take my bearings from them!

The 1981 race, of course, represented the turning point in my career fortunes with an invitation to drive the Jules-sponsored Porsche 936. As I have already said, we hardly touched the thing throughout the 24 hours and, once again with Jacky Ickx, breezed through to secure my second win and his third.

In 1982 we took the 956 to Le Mans for the first time. I shared with Jacky again, it by now becoming clear that he and I had built up a technical and strategic rapport for this endurance racing business. In a nutshell, we had managed to put our finger on the recipe for success and there was no question that some of Jacky's legendary luck was beginning to rub off on me!

Familiar sight! On the victory rostrum with Jacky Ickx after winning Le Mans with the Jules Porsche 936 in 1981. We came back to score our third win together the following year with the Rothmans Porsche 956, then missed our hat trick in '83 by less than half a minute. **Below** *Out on the circuit with the winning car which did not miss a beat all through the 1981 race.*

Jacky took the start and grabbed an immediate lead, but we were delayed in the early stages with a fuel mixture problem which dropped us back a bit. Vern was in the second works entry with Jochen Mass and they ran into rev limiter trouble during that opening phase, so our additional back-up entry, driven by Al Holbert, Hurley Haywood and Porsche engineer Jürgen Barth took the chance to lead early on.

Ickx and I got our heads down to pull back that early deficit and, after the leaders suffered wheel bearing trouble and Holbert lost a driver's door on the Mulsanne straight, we got back into the lead at about one o'clock on Sunday morning. From that moment onwards it was a re-run of 1981. The car didn't miss a beat and we cruised home to win from Vern and Jochen, with the other car recovering to third place to make it a Rothmans Porsche grand slam.

If '82 was routine, the 1983 Le Mans outing was an absolute epic, although Jacky and I failed to pick up another victory. On the second lap of the race, Jan Lammers in the Canon Porsche 956 was dicing for the lead with Ickx and managed to take him off at the end of the Mulsanne straight. Jacky spun without serious damage, but it could have been a lot worse, happening as it did right in front of the pack.

It took us a 14-hour slog to get back into the lead and, at six o'clock on Sunday morning, I slipstreamed past Schuppan on the Mulsanne straight to take over at the front of the field – briefly! Seconds later, as I accelerated through Mulsanne corner, the engine cut out! I managed to lift up the huge engine cover and fix the problem, but it lost us a lot of time and we were also hampered by cracked brake discs.

Vern, meanwhile, was having trouble in the 962 he was sharing with Al Holbert and Hurley Haywood. He lost his nearside door, again on the Mulsanne straight, in what amounted to a repeat of Holbert's problem the previous year. He came back slowly for repairs, but the airflow over the rear of the car had been disrupted, with the result that one of the water-cooled cylinder heads had got very hot indeed and the engine began to seize during the last hour.

At about that time Norbert Singer came to get me to take over from Ickx, although by that time I was so brassed off that I felt like letting Jacky take it through to the finish. As Ickx got out of the car he said, 'The brakes have absolutely had it'. So Singer said, 'What do we do? Either change the discs, which will take ten minutes? Or you drive slowly?' I decided to go for it and, brakes or no brakes, broke the lap record several times in the final hour. But we just failed to win our Le Mans hat-trick!

Going into the last lap, poor Al Holbert was absolutely terrified when the leading car momentarily seized solid, but somehow it managed to limp round to take the chequered flag first. I did absolutely everything I could, but was still just 20 s or so behind at the end. As I've explained, by now Vern was out of the works team on a regular basis and had been signed only for Le Mans, to drive the third car. For once he'd had some luck, but I hadn't been with him to benefit on this rare occasion!

Going into the last lap, Al Holbert was absolutely terrified when the leading car momentarily seized solid.

The 1984 Group C season was beset by problems which resulted in the Porsche factory team missing Le Mans altogether. Ever since Group C had been introduced in 1982, FISA had been keen to achieve a situation where sports car racing on both sides of the Atlantic was run to the same technical regulations. However, the IMSA series promoters and organizers were not terribly interested in picking up the fuel economy aspect of the World Sports Car Championship – rightly, in my view – and when FISA announced that the 1984 WSC rules would restrict fuel capacity by another 15 per cent the gap between the two categories seemed to be wider than ever.

Porsche obviously spent an enormous amount of time, effort and money working with Bosch on a complex new engine management system which would keep the 956s competitive. Six weeks before the season began, FISA then dropped its bombshell. Out of the blue, it anounced that the 15 per cent fuel reduction would be scrapped and, for 1985, the World Sports Car Championship would adopt a variation on the IMSA regulations whereby performance would be governed by an engine capacity/weight formula. FISA also said that the cars would have to comply with the IMSA constructional regulations, most importantly that the driver's feet should be placed behind the front wheel centre line.

At a stroke, the Porsche 956 and the Lancia LC2 would be outdated and illegal. Porsche, understandably, were enraged. They chose to make their dissatisfaction public by withdrawing the works team from Le Mans, leaving the way open for one of the Joest team 956s to sustain Porsche's winning reputation. Naturally, for we factory drivers it was a great disappointment, but eventually FISA produced some compromise technical regulations which got every-body back on the road in 1985, moderately satisfied.

With the new Porsche 962, which conformed to the revised footbox regulations, we could only finish third at Le Mans, outdis-tanced by the Canon and Joest team private entries. I was now sharing with my regular team-mate Hans Stuck and, although we lost some time with a seized wheel bearing, we were no match for those private entries in terms of fuel consumption because they had done their homework better.

The arrival of Jaguar on the scene in 1986 certainly perked up interest in the endurance racing scene, but it wasn't until 1987 that

On the way to third place at Le Mans, beaten by a couple of Porsche privateers who had done their sums more accurately than the works team!

the English cars were developed to the point where they could make a serious bid for victory at Le Mans. Although I won my fourth victory there in 1986, by far my most satisfying success was in the 1987 race where, for the second straight year, I shared with both Hans Stuck and Al Holbert.

Prior to Le Mans, Jaguar expended an enormous amount of effort running endurance tests at Paul Ricard and generally making it very clear that their cars would be capable of making a truly effective challenge in the bid to topple Porsche from its usual place on the rostrum. We already knew that we were fighting an uphill battle with the Porsche 962 chassis, which was clearly no longer a match for the more modern cars from Tom Walkinshaw's impressive stable. We also appreciated that our engines were not quite as fuel efficient as the 7-litre Jaguar V12s but, equally, that Jaguar's successes had been achieved up to that point only in six-hour, 1,000 km races. Dress rehearsals perhaps, but Le Mans was the real thing. Now they had to run four times that distance against the team that knew how to get the job done.

The run-up to Le Mans, and indeed the early stages of the race, were fraught by any standards for the Porsche team. Stuck crashed one of our cars at the Weissach test track, then American driver Price Cobb wrote off what was supposed to be the third factory race entry during practice. Come the race, Jochen retired the pole-position 956 with a burned piston caused by incompatibility between the fuel supplied by the organizers and the micro-chip in the car's engine management system.

Naturally, Hans and I were very worried by this, and we had a long stop to have our management system fitted with a more suitable micro-chip before our engine went the same way. Within two hours of the start, there were still three Jaguars to beat out there and we

Start of Le Mans in 1986 with the two works Rothmans 962s being swallowed up by a couple of privateers and one of the new Jags already pressing hard. A day later, however, we were convincingly on top, as this shot of Stuck, Holbert and myself on the rostrum underlines only too well!

were the only surviving works Porsche. During those early hours I was screwed up with concern. I kept asking our engineers, 'Is it going to go wrong for us?' But it wasn't until later in the evening that I began to feel confident that we would last to the finish. More than that, I began to get a sniff of another win. The Jaguars were fast and threatening, but they had still to prove themselves in a 24-hour battle. The odds may have been stacked against us, three to one, in purely mathematical terms. But we began to feel increasingly confident as the night wore on. As the Jaguars hit trouble, one by one, the pressure came off us and went on to them!

Saturday evening was enlivened for me by a great race with Martin Brundle in one of the Jaguars. We drove extremely hard and had a great time, 'drafting' each other down the Mulsanne straight and really working the cars. I haven't had so much sheer fun for a long time. By the time I got on terms with him again, on the Sunday morning, our Porsche was four laps in the lead and I didn't really want to get embroiled in a scrap. On the other hand, I didn't want him to get away from me either, because that four-lap advantage could soon have been whittled down to three laps and, almost unconsciously, we might have slackened the pace to the point where we became vulnerable.

Saturday evening was enlivened by a great race with Martin Brundle. I haven't had so much sheer fun for a long time.

So I just kept with him, not allowing him to disappear out of sight. Then I began to notice a tell-tale pencil of smoke coming from the Jaguar and realized there was no way it would last the remaining nine hours. Three laps later he stopped with engine failure . . .

I always thought it would take Walkinshaw three years to 'massage' those Jaguars into winning propositions and, while none of them made it to the finish in 1986, at least in 1987 they kept one running long enough to finish fifth, although it was a long way behind after a whole bag of problems. I am sure that they will be out to make it 'third time lucky' in 1988, so I will be looking forward to that race with even more than usual anticipation.

We drove as fast as we could in 1987, forcing the Jaguars to get embroiled in a fight. To be honest, we forced the pace rather than taking things easy and hanging about behind them, hoping they would break. They were slightly more fuel-efficient than our Porsche, but Hans and I knew that there is always a pace car period at some time or another during a race as long as Le Mans which enables you to get your consumption back on schedule if you have gone slightly over the limit.

Getting serious. The new TWR Jaguar XJR-6s in amongst, and here briefly leading, our Porsche 962s at Le Mans in 1986.

Not that ours was a trouble-free run by any means: we did have a few problems to deal with while battling with those Jaguars. The Porsche's turbo boost gauge packed up early in the race, so I took over the car not knowing what sort of boost level we were running for about six hours. Then the battery managed to flatten itself while we were following the pace car and we changed it again later. In addition to that, the windscreen seemed to have worked loose and was rattling round for much of the race, allowing rain to leak in round the edges to trickle across the glass on the inside. We had suffered that problem in practice, but never quite managed to work out where it was coming from. Initially, I thought it must be coming in through the door, somehow, but we discovered otherwise when we knuckled down to the race itself!

Aside from the success, there was one aspect of the weekend which slightly took the edge off our elation. Two hours before the end, when Hans was out on the circuit driving the car, Professor Bott told me the team would be withdrawing from the championship for the rest of the season and that the Porsche factory would not be contesting a full programme of Sports Car Championship races in 1988. So, before we had finished winning the 1987 race, the decision had been taken that no factory Porsche would be seen again in a major international endurance race until Le Mans in 1988. I must say, when he told me I had my mind on the race itself and the news didn't fully sink in. Also, I was absolutely amazed that nobody at Porsche got round to telling Hans about the decision for another week.

It was a hard decision to accept. I found myself facing the 1988 season in potentially the same state as I was when I drove for Renault at Le Mans only in 1977 and '78. How can you put together a season-long deal with another team without including the most important event on the sports car calendar? It's just not realistic, so Hans and I were left with the choice of throwing up our commitment to the works team and finding a regular seat with a private team, or keeping the faith with Porsche for Le Mans and bumping along on a race-by-race basis with other outfits, where possible, for the rest of the year.

Le Mans is a very individualistic sort of place, in some ways trading on its glittering reputation and rather reluctant to instigate much in the way of change and improvement to the circuit. The circuit has changed considerably over the years, on a long-term basis, but I always come away with the impression that the organizers may have listened to what you say, but they're not really interested in acting on it. They privately take the view, 'Oh, if he doesn't come back and race here next year, then somebody else will'. In that respect we have a problem because there is no united front amongst the drivers and teams that can get on terms with the Le Mans organizers. OSCAR, the organization of sports car racing entrants, has done a fine job in many respects, but it doesn't carry much in the way of clout at Le Mans. There are just too many entrants keen to do Le Mans and no other race.

I must say, I have mixed feelings about the place. On the one hand I agree with Bob Wollek, who really laid into the organizers at a press conference just before the 1987 race, accusing them of being too casual over their attitudes towards safety improvements. But on the other hand I tend to think, hold on one minute, in 1971 we hurtled down the Mulsanne straight at 245 mph with our feet sticking out ahead of the front axle, no sponge-filled fuel tanks and so on. We tend to forget that we were all happy to race there back in those days. I'm not saying we can't improve things, but there must be some degree of balance between taking risks and being paranoid about safety.

I'm not saying we can't improve things, but there must be some degree of balance between taking risks and being paranoid about safety.

Of course, if you equate things in purely financial terms, then you can quite easily conclude that Le Mans isn't worth the effort, particularly when you take into account the safety factor. Harsh reality being what it is, some people might think that it's worth taking a gamble at somewhere like Indianapolis, for example, where the winner can walk away with £300,000. But for the £12,000 earned by the winning car at Le Mans in 1987, you begin to wonder. Out of that, *all* the works drivers in *all* the works cars get an equal share-out!

The organizers' attitude is based on their fundamental belief that Le Mans is a great race which will always attract a huge crowd, whatever sort of cars are raced there. That's as maybe, but they should really take a long-term view. For example, those old pits really need replacing so that a wider pit lane can be provided. Ultimately, the over-crowding can be dealt with by restricting the number of people permitted in the pits. That's the organizers' problem. But it would help the competitors if the whole area was modernized up to the standards which are now taken totally for granted in Formula 1.

There are other areas as well where their priorities have become confused. For example, that new S-bend just beyond the right-hander after the pits is a complete joke. It's an awful corner. And when did the last car crash there? Years ago. They did it for the motor cycles, to prevent them from becoming airborne over the crest just beyond. But they haven't blended it back on to the main circuit at the optimum angle, so it's quite a tricky corner and, in my view, an unnecessary one.

Another bee in people's bonnets tends to concern speeds on the Mulsanne straight. Aside from Win Percy's 1987 shunt in the Jaguar, which was caused almost certainly by a tyre deflation, most of the accidents in the past have occurred long before the cars have reached anywhere near their maximum speed. But Mulsanne is perceived as being a dangerous section of the track. The truth of the matter is that the narrow, tree-lined section from the end of the Mulsanne straight down towards Indianapolis corner frightens me stiff. There's not much room to pass and the speed differentials are every bit as bad. That is the section on which Jo Bonnier was killed in 1972, his Lola flying over the barrier into the trees after colliding with a slower Ferrari Daytona.

The narrow, tree-lined section from the end of the Mulsanne straight down towards Indianapolis corner frightens me stiff.

Memories of that accident bring into focus another crucially worrying aspect of these endurance races – the wide disparity of performance amongst the cars and drivers. The problem, of course, is how on earth does one find 120 drivers of sufficient experience and ability to handle the sort of cars we are racing at Le Mans? I believe that the entry qualifications for a race like Le Mans should be far more stringent than they are at present, requiring a certain number of finishes in six-hour/1,000 km events beforehand. That way, at least you could be certain that they had some idea of what they were up against from the point of view of speed differentials and potential fatigue.

Le Mans has been romanticized beyond belief by many people, but the truth is that it's not romantic at all. It's hellishly demanding, gruelling and exhausting. Grand Prix drivers may dismiss it as an uncompetitive side-show, but while agreeing that sports car racing is nowhere near so competitive as Formula 1, I can assure the doubters that Le Mans is different. Those Formula 1 aces who are used to an hour and a half of flat-out sprint racing might find it considerably more difficult than they think if they came and tried their hand at the Sarthe in a competitive and reliable car!

Chapter 5

The endurance racing technique

To start with, how does one define an endurance race? It's my personal feeling that only the two 24-hour races at Daytona and Le Mans are really endurance races in the true sense of the word. I don't, for example, regard either three- or six-hour races in the same class. It's interesting to reflect that today's World Championship Grands Prix are regarded as hard work at around an hour and a half, but in the sports car world we regard a race twice that length as a sprint!

The basis of my fitness, or otherwise, has its roots in diet and detailed preparation. I make a big effort to keep in good shape and have quite a rigid regime which I stick to in the height of the season. My personal schedule is also complicated by the problems produced by jet lag. With an extensive programme of sports car races on both sides of the Atlantic throughout 1987, often on alternating weekends, I made around 30 trans-Atlantic flights that year and, indeed, I have done for the past few seasons. Consequently, I have made a lot of effort to understand the way my body behaves and to try to treat it sympathetically.

Every businessman suffers from jet lag, even if he doesn't acknowledge it. For the sportsman it can be a really major problem, so I have taken a lot of advice, and read a great deal, as to how I can come to terms with it. The most interesting source of material I found in a document published by the US Olympic Commission which concluded that, ideally, you need to allow one full day to recover for every hour the time zone changes. Quite clearly, that's just not possible with my schedule because, when I travel to most American races, I tend to leave England on the Wednesday or Thursday for a race on the Sunday. If I followed that rule of thumb, a five-hour time change would take until the following Tuesday before it was squeezed out of my system. So, quite obviously, I try to work out a reasonable compromise.

If I go out to the east coast of America on a Wednesday, the following morning I feel a bit like a wet rag. It's different to being purely a businessman because a businessman can remain on European time if he likes, but a sportsman who is taking part in a specific event at a specific time just hasn't that facility. In practical terms, by the time race morning comes round on the Sunday, I'm feeling pretty fit. But then there is the problem of returning to the UK to be faced, losing that five hours coming back across the Atlantic. In that case, I always try to stay up as long as possible, go to bed at what would normally be the correct time and perhaps take half a sleeping tablet, just to make certain I don't find myself waking up at four o'clock in the morning.

Tennis is great for the cardio-vascular system, although it's not every day you get a chance to play opposite Martina Navratilova!

I've always liked to think of myself as a bit of a dab-hand at football . . .

Of course, the North Atlantic trip is a side-show compared with the crushing nine-hour time difference to Japan, where most people in racing confess to having terrible problems with jet lag. With a five-hour time difference, at least you are racing in what will still be daylight back home. In Japan, you are racing at something like four o'clock in the morning. That takes an enormous amount out of you because, although you can fool your personal body clock to a small extent, you can't trick it sufficiently to feel really good under those circumstances.

I have also thrived on my various sports ever since I left school, but I now find my business diary so full that I really have to make a tremendous effort to make time for them. I play squash and field hockey, and go swimming as often as possible. Swimming is great for the cardio-vascular system and doesn't put damage on your body in the same way as running, which wears out your joints.

Chris Amon used to say, 'Derek, the day you can beat me on the track I'll start to take physical training seriously'.

There is no underestimating the importance of fitness in a sport as physically punishing as professional motor racing. Others are rather more cynical about the amount of effort needed to work yourself into physical shape. I remember when we were all out in Australia and New Zealand doing the Tasman series almost 20 years ago we all swam, and played squash and tennis together, but Chris Amon used to say, 'Derek, the day you can beat me on the track will be the day that I'll start to take physical training seriously'. Well, we all know that Chris didn't need to prove anything on the track. He was a brilliant driver, true enough, but I always reflect back to that remark and wonder just how good and successful he might have been had he taken training seriously, cut back on his chain-smoking and just tried to get himself fit.

I believe that physical fitness and determination can go a long way towards bridging the gap between the driver who is talented and the one who is really brilliant. For example, I never believed myself to be on the same level as Jochen Rindt or Ronnie Peterson, but I'm sure that by being very fit I have been able to close the gap separating us on occasion. Where they have tailed off, fitness-wise, during a race, I have been able to maintain my effort to the finish.

Keke Rosberg's theory is that the best possible training for driving a racing car is driving a racing car.

I've heard about Keke Rosberg's theory that the best possible training for driving a racing car is just that, driving a racing car, and I suppose that's all right as far as it goes. But, as I've said before, an hour and 40 minutes in a Grand Prix car isn't quite the same thing as keeping motivated, physically and mentally, throughout one's driving stints in an endurance race. Basically, though, Keke is right. If I could do a 1,000 km race every fortnight, plus a bit of testing in between, I reckon that would keep me pretty fit.

One thing, though, in connection with Amon and Rosberg, I don't care what you say, a person who smokes can never be as fit as a guy who doesn't, and that applies to racing drivers every bit as much as any professional sportsman. The functioning of your cardio-vascular system is absolutely of paramount importance to a racing driver. If you can't breathe deeply and absorb sufficient oxygen for the job in hand, then you just won't have the stamina or ability to concentrate for long periods.

I am fortunate in that I have an amazing ability to absorb oxygen, so, although I perspire a great deal, I have lots of stamina. That's crucially important in an endurance race, more so at Daytona even than at Le Mans, as I'll come back and explain later.

I also spend a lot of time in the gym when I'm home, working out with weights, and I run a good deal as well. A year or two ago I was put through a series of physiological tests at Montreal's McGill University, which had also run tests on Grand Prix drivers such as Martin Brundle, Derek Warwick and Jonathan Palmer, presumably when they had been in town for the Canadian Grand Prix. In many areas I was right on a par with them in terms of fitness, something I didn't think was bad when you consider that I'm 15 years older than them all!

While I was there, somebody said, 'By the way, have you read *Eat to Win*, by Dr Robert Haas?' I said I'd never heard of it, so one of the people there popped over the road to a bookshop and got me a copy there and then. It makes fascinating reading, detailing which components in your diet are really important, explaining that when you sweat it is not just water that you lose, but minerals, electrolytes and so on, as well as telling you why the body needs all these substances and what it does with them.

There are many misconceptions about dietary requirements for those expending a lot of physical energy. There are those who believe that the best way to set yourself up for an endurance race is a large steak at the start of the day. But the truth of the matter is that the body uses a great deal of energy actually digesting food, so when you are wound up tight under the competitive conditions which exist at a motor race your body doesn't want to be faced with the task of using all that energy to work at digesting a heavy meal. At Le Mans in the past I was introduced to a fully balanced liquid food called Sustagen, which proved ideal in that it gave me all the replenishment my system needed, without any of the bulk.

I had not appreciated just how important carbohydrates are to your system. In order to digest proteins you use up a great deal of water, and carbohydrates do a great job in that they store water. That is why many athletes find pasta so effective as a means of 'carbohydrate loading' which, in turn, will help their water retention under pressure. As an example, the body uses up about three cups of its own water in the process of consuming one cup of coffee. Replacing that water effectively is not a great priority in normal life on a day-to-day basis, but it is important when the pressure is on.

Having said all that, I don't think I'm cranky about what I eat, even away at a long-distance race. The first year I really gave any serious consideration to my diet was in 1985 and, as a result, I must admit that I seemed to avoid the inevitable colds and flu which do the rounds every winter. Nowadays I'm a little more relaxed about it all, but I'm still quite cautious. I mean, I don't sit around the place drinking a glass of water and nibbling an apple four times a day. But I seriously believe that the body needs a balanced diet, so I steer clear of butter and milk, eat a lot of vegetables and am pretty cautious about beef.

That's how I approach the business of endurance racing from the physical standpoint, after which success depends to an extent on a complex blend of sheer good luck and shrewd experience. When people talk to me about luck, I always have to think very carefully. Of course, when you're talking about a race which is as long as 24 hours, an element of luck must always come into the equation. But it is a bit too straightforward for any success to be attributed solely to that. I believe it's luck up to a point, but it must be more than that.

Primarily, to be a successful endurance driver requires a considerable amount of mechanical sympathy, in addition to the ability to run the car as hard and as fast as it will go for as long as is required. You will be called upon to drive the car to the limit of its performance, but

I perspire a great deal when racing, so fluid retention is clearly a high priority for me . . .

you must manage that without over-stressing it. That is not always as straightforward as you might imagine.

On many occasions people have said to me, 'You're lucky, winning four or five Le Mans races'. I don't usually get involved in a debate with people like this. I usually just walk away. I think once or twice might be fairly lucky, but by the time you've won a race like Le Mans five times, obviously a great deal more than luck has entered into it.

Take Jochen Mass, for example. He is a driver for whom I have considerable respect and admiration. Yet he has never won Le Mans, even though he has driven a car which has been identical to mine. When things go wrong, I always find myself saying 'bad luck' to Jochen, but I'm not sure I believe it's my 'good luck' that I win any more than it is his bad luck that he loses. To some extent it's a question of compatibility between team-mates, between drivers and the car. It's not something that is easy to put your finger on, but there has to be an elusive reason why he's had exactly the same car as me at Le Mans for the past six or seven years, yet hasn't once won the race.

Taking that sort of fortune to an even more ironic level, when I

won the 1987 Le Mans race with Stuck and Holbert we were actually using the car originally earmarked for Wollek and Mass. We had two cars written off before the race, so Jochen and Bob took ours and we were switched to the 962 originally down to be driven by Vern Schuppan and Price Cobb. And the car was superb, really as good as anything I've ever driven in that race. I can only believe that Stuck, Holbert and I make the best driving partnership. There has to be a reason, not only for my five Le Mans wins, but also the fact that in my last six visits to Daytona I've scored four second places and two wins. At the end of the day, you have to say that the drivers must have done one hell of a job!

I wish I could pin-point what has made me such an effective long-distance driver. I was never taught by anybody how to pace myself, going right back to that maddening outing in the works Ferrari in 1970. I don't ever remember having any particular problems coming to terms with endurance racing techniques and, I suppose, I've been fortunate that I have raced with so many compatible drivers. I don't recall ever having to alter my mental outlook in any way. I just slipped into the business helped, perhaps,

Melanie helps her Dad to top up during a break from the cockpit on the way to victory in 1987.

by the fact that I was partnered with an immensely experienced and very talented man in the shape of Jo Siffert during that fledgeling season with the JW Gulf Porsches in 1971. Both he and Jacky Ickx taught me a great deal about having the right temperament, because balancing your individual ambitions with the requirements of an overall team effort can be quite complicated. Endurance racing teams have no room for mavericks who want to buck the system and do their own thing.

Endurance racing teams have no room for mavericks who want to buck the system and do their own thing.

A great deal of debate has gone on over the years as to which of the great 24-hour classic races is the most demanding—Le Mans or Daytona. They both call for tremendous discipline and stamina, but I firmly believe that Daytona is far and away more challenging and wearing than its famous French counterpart. Daytona is a race where three drivers are a necessity, rather than an option, and when I was part of the winning team there in 1987 a total of four drivers actually had a turn behind the wheel during the 24 hours.

Daytona is far away more challenging and wearing than its famous French counterpart.

The great thing that enables you to relax at Le Mans is the Mulsanne straight. I'm talking about 'relax' in relative terms, of course, but that 3½-mile straight, at full throttle in fifth gear, at least gives you a chance to relax your muscles slightly, move your shoulders around, flex your wrists and generally de-cramp yourself.

Daytona, by comparison, offers no such luxury and is therefore much more difficult. Casual enthusiasts believe that it must be quite an easy race, slamming round the banking for lap after lap, but they are mistakenly thinking about the NASCAR Grand National saloon car races. During the sports car endurance events we brake heavily immediately after the pits, before scrabbling round a second-gear left-hander into a nerve-racking sequence of very tight corners, usually crowded with cars of widely varying performance potential. When I first went there, in 1971, it was possible to relax ever so slightly on the back straight – if hurtling towards the banking at 190 mph in a Porsche 917 can be called relaxing—your vision round the banking hopefully enhanced at that speed by special perspex slots let into the roof panels, enabling you to see further round the banking than you would otherwise be able to.

Now there is the added problem of a tight chicane just before you accelerate out on to the banking and, because they are reluctant to make anything permanent in case it causes problems for any wayward NASCAR saloon, the kerbing is makeshift and unsatisfactory. Slower cars drop their wheels over the kerbing, kicking stones and dirt back on to the track. So you come whistling through in your Porsche 962, hit the 'marbles' and then spend the next couple of laps round the banking secretly worrying whether in fact you might have picked up a slow puncture. Tyre failure on the banking at Daytona is definitely something you can do without!

The G-loadings involved there are truly punishing. Add to that the lack of any let-up and you can understand that, when a driver change was scheduled for our Lowenbrau Porsche two hours from the end of the 1987 race, we had something of a problem on our hands. One of the 962's side windows had been sucked out, ruining the cockpit ventilation and making life extremely uncomfortable. Al Unser Jr was sick, Chip Robinson didn't have the strength to climb into the car and I was suffering quite badly from cramps. Thankfully, Al Holbert had been togged up as crew chief, ready to go, for most of the race, waiting for just such an eventuality, and he took over the car for an hour and a half. By then, A. J. Foyt's pursuing Porsche had blown its engine after he had screwed the boost pressure up too high trying to catch us. At that stage we were only 24 s apart after 23 hours, so we were left with an easy run to victory and Al handed it back to me for the final sprint to the flag.

At the point where Al took over from me, I really thought I was finished for the day. I went and lay down in the motorhome and could hardly move for the cramp. The team masseur was trying to keep my muscles under control when a mechanic popped his head round the door and said, 'You're on in 15 minutes'. So I tried, with assistance, to get my overalls on, but every time I moved, the muscular spasms started. At that point the mechanic reappeared and said, 'He's coming in on the next lap,' and I instinctively bent down, did up my shoes, ran across the paddock and leapt into the car. A surge of adrenalin had taken over from the cramp and I never had any more trouble that day!

Any Grand Prix driver who makes a habit of getting involved in first-lap tangles will probably be wasting his time at Le Mans or Daytona.

Discipline is of enormous importance to the endurance racer. You need to be psyched up at the start, but not carried away with the enthusiasm of the moment. Any Grand Prix driver, for example, who makes a habit of getting involved in first-lap tangles will probably be wasting his time at Le Mans or Daytona. If you don't take the first driving stint at the start, in some ways you feel curiously detached from the action, but it's important to maintain your mental balance.

That's particularly important at Le Mans, not because it's such a long race or so bloody dangerous, but because you get caught up in the glamour, colour and tension of the occasion. Formula 1 folk may take that for granted in their world, but it's something that we only experience at Le Mans in Europe and at a couple of other races in North America. You must not let that tension get to you.

Curiously, I feel relaxed about my personal prospects, but fairly tense on behalf of my co-driver if I'm not taking the start. Stuck and Ickx have usually done the first stint during my partnerships with them, so I find watching the early laps a fairly nerve-racking affair. But when I take my turn behind the wheel I am totally relaxed because the race has already settled down into a pattern and the initial excitement has died away.

It doesn't bother me at all letting my co-driver take the start. All through my time at Le Mans I've always said that I'd rather be in the car at the finish, if there's a choice, and it is an arrangement I've always stuck to with Jacky Ickx.

Strapped in, almost ready to go, prior to the long slog!

The right co-driver for the best result. Unquestionably, some of Jack Ickx's good fortune rubbed off on me. From left to right in this 1981 Le Mans Group: Catherine Ickx, Justin, Melanie, me, Pam, Jacky Ickx and (holding hat) Ferry Porsche.

When Jacky came into the Gulf team for Le Mans in 1975 he was most deferential towards me, acknowledging that I had done all the development work on the Mirage and, accordingly, being prepared to take what was effectively a number-two role. I said, 'Well, as it's my car, in effect, I'd like to do the start,' and he agreed. Then, when it was clear that we were winning, I said, 'To be honest, after all this effort I would like to take the finish'. And Ickx didn't raise one murmur of objection.

He never said a word and, when I came in to join him in the Porsche for 1981, he said simply, 'I'll start and I'd like you to finish'. He felt that we should both share any success that was coming our way, so he would take the hype at the start and I would be allowed the prestige of the finish, particularly if it turned out to be a win. Since then, I've always had a similar arrangement with all my co-drivers and it seems to have worked well.

This chapter is about the endurance racing technique, but I still find myself pondering this question of luck. Perhaps, when you analyse things, there is an element of good fortune in getting involved with the most suitable team-mate. In my heart, I tend to believe that you make your own luck, but if that's the case then some of Jacky's seems to have rubbed off on me. As I've said before in my comments about Vern Schuppan, I just felt uncomfortable not being with Jacky. It wasn't so much that I was concerned about my own bad luck, it was that I knew Ickx had good luck, so I wanted to be around to share in it. We just clicked when we drove together. It's the same with Hans

The endurance racing team; Porsche knows the technique better than most. Unfortunately, Jacky Ickx is missing from this official team photograph.

Stuck and Al Holbert. The chemistry seems to be correct and always works well. You may have the best technical equipment in the business, but unless you have a sympathetic driving team the results won't flow. This is one of the totally intangible facets of endurance racing.

In the early stages of an endurance event it's necessary to balance speed with the necessity to conserve the car. Blazing a trail at the front of the field is all very entertaining, but it doesn't necessarily mean you are going to win. It is often better to run with the leading bunch, but not necessarily be the pace-setter. That way you can weigh up the opposition quite accurately without showing too much of your own hand. Keeping in touch, while keeping out of trouble, is the ideal at which to aim.

Pit stops, of course, assume a slightly different priority to those in Formula 1. We've all watched in admiration as Ferrari or McLaren mechanics change four wheels in seven seconds, enabling their man to dash back into a Grand Prix sprint without losing half-a-dozen places. In endurance racing terms, it simply doesn't matter that much. There is no sense in risking a loose wheel, for example, simply to gain ten seconds in a 24-hour thrash.

Endurance racing pit stops tend to be slick, but undramatic. I've got used to their controlled tempo and, of course, the Porsche factory mechanics have polished their technique into a good blend of speed and efficiency. From the public's point of view, it's all very amusing to have wheels flying all over the place, but it doesn't do a great deal for the drivers' nerves. Certainly, in the Le Mans pit road there is just no way you can carry out a really quick stop because

Right *You need to demonstrate mechanical sympathy in a reliable car; the Jules-backed Porsche 936 which Ickx and I used to win Le Mans in 1981 was new for the race, yet never missed a beat all the way to the flag.*

Below *Hans Stuck picked up where Jacky Ickx left off as one of my most successful teammates. For some reason, we just clicked together and the results flowed.*

there's scarcely room to walk round the car, let alone flick surplus wheels over your shoulder!

As far as I'm concerned, once I've wound down slightly from the pace out on the circuit, I'm happy that the mechanics take time to ensure everything is fixed or attached properly. I want them to check that the wheel nuts are done up. If the windscreen is loose, I want to know that they can spend two minutes trying to fix it, rather than thinking to myself, 'Oh God, I'm not going to mention that to them because they're going to take three minutes to do it'. Having a calm, measured pit stop is a good opportunity for the driver to take a break, compose himself and take stock of the situation, even for half a minute.

The ability to pace yourself is also a major factor influencing a driver's effectiveness throughout a long-distance race. During a six-hour event, for example, there seems to be a sort of 'no man's land' after three hours which becomes something of a psychological low point, particularly if you are not involved in a race with a rival. First time in the car everybody is fresh, and the adrenalin is flowing, but by this stage the initial euphoria has worn off and there is still a long way to go to the chequered flag. That middle spell often seems to drift away into obscurity in the back of your memory and is something difficult to recall when the race is over.

People ask me whether it's depressing, lapping steadily and alone in the middle of a long-distance sports car race, almost as if we're just sitting there cruising around at six-tenths waiting for somebody to wave the chequered flag. Of course, it's not like that at all, because we are actually trying to race. The one restricting factor which really upsets me, of course, is this question of fuel consumption limitations.

At somewhere like Le Mans this can pose quite a nerve-racking

Least appealing aspect of endurance racing in the 1980s has been the fuel consumption formula. Here Ickx and I struggle to eke out our fuel load to the finish of the 1982 Silverstone 1,000 km, the Porsche 956's maiden outing and one of the most frustrating races of my career.

incidental problem. In the cockpit you have to keep your eye on a fuel computer while at the same time reading off a card which itemizes how the fuel consumption should progress during a given stint at the wheel. Each time past the pits you check that you haven't consumed more than the allotted amount and, if you have, it's quite simply a question of easing back on the Mulsanne straight in order to get the figures back on target again.

The sheer frustration of being dictated to by a fuel computer has been the single most aggravating aspect of endurance racing over the past decade. Having said that, the self-discipline it imposes is quite remarkable. It's rather like having the sword of Damocles hanging over your head. Sure, you can turn up the boost pressure and be the fastest car on the track. But you won't make it to the finish. It is one of my pet abominations which I get extremely angry about when I so much as spend a second thinking about that absurd situation we found ourselves in back in 1982, at the Silverstone 1,000 km.

I'll never forget cruising the whole lap at Silverstone in fifth gear for as long as I live; it was one of the most supremely frustrating moments of my entire racing career. We qualified around the 1 m 18 s mark and were obliged to lap about seven seconds slower in order to get to the finish. I strongly believe that we are abusing the paying public, putting on shows of that sort, and without the public there wouldn't be any racing. That sort of self-discipline from a naturally competitive driver is often hard to muster. Very hard indeed.

Of course, the Porsche endurance driver in the turbo era has to deal with the gamesmanship which is inevitably produced as a by-product of fiddling around with the boost pressure control in the cockpit. A lot has been written and rumoured about various drivers, but I've never been totally certain which of my colleagues has wound the boost right off the dial during qualifying in order to set a quick time.

One of the biggest problems with this technique is that you are invariably risking damage to the engine you've got to race the following day, but there is an element of bluff and double-bluff which is interesting to keep an eye on. During qualifying, a driver might use 1.55-bar boost pressure, set a quick time and then roll into the pits where he will reply, casually, '1.4-bar' to any rival asking him what boost level he was running. We all do it to some extent. It's human nature.

Jockeying for position in traffic, one must balance competitive urgency with the need to keep the car intact and out of unnecessary trouble.

When it comes to the race, the fuel consumption constraints come into play again. Some drivers use a bit too much fuel during their stint at the wheel, leaving their team-mates with the problem of eking out slightly less than their apparent allocation of fuel to cover the same distance. I've done it once or twice and it's certainly been done to me

by a couple of my team-mates. Again, it's gamesmanship, but in the ultimate analysis there's not much point in going like a madman, way over the limit, because at the end of the day you are jeopardizing your own chances of finishing the race.

Rounding off my objection to this ridiculous form of motor racing, it should be emphasized that the fuel consumption regulations oblige sports car drivers to adopt a dramatically different driving style. Take Stowe corner at Silverstone, for example. You back off at 250 metres, go hard on the brakes at 150 metres and then scramble round the corner without losing too much speed, your turbo boost dropping away all the time. That's a depressing contrast to the more conventional technique you can adopt during qualifying, braking hard at, say, 175 metres, changing down, braking again and then driving round in one smooth, satisfying sweep.

The performance differential between qualifying and the race also tends to affect the car's handling. Set the car up in qualifying and it feels quite nice, but running three seconds off the pace during the race, a 962 feels like a truck. If we could use that 'hidden' extra 50 bhp in the race, we could kick the tail out, tuck the nose in towards the apex and get through the corners the way the car was originally designed to!

One of the most wearing aspects of endurance racing is the variation in car performance you encounter on the track and, as a result, you must always remain alert to the possibility of some relative novice in a slower car lurching across your bows from time to time. That is the sort of occasion on which you have to judge whether to barge through inside at the last moment under braking, or simply wait until he has gone through the corner before accelerating by afterwards.

I was really getting the hang of one of the most crucial corners on the track, the 190 mph Masta kink.

My most vivid recollection of such a problem came during practice for the 1972 Spa 1,000 km race when I was driving one of the Gulf Mirages. It was the first day of qualifying and I was really thrashing along hard, dicing with Ickx in the Ferrari 312P. We were fairly evenly matched and I was really getting the hang of one of the most crucial corners on the track, the 190 mph Masta kink which was a flat-out left-right between a couple of houses.

Prior to the first day of qualifying I had been told that the son of a senior European Gulf executive was competing in the race in one of the smaller 2-litre cars, but I did not think any more about it. In the first session I went slamming into the Masta kink and, just as I turned in, my eyes caught a 2-litre car which was going so slowly that I

Hurtling through Stavelot with the Gulf Mirage during qualifying for the 1972 Spa 1,000 km – shortly before that enormous moment in the Masta kink where a slower car caused me to take to the grass. Thankfully, as you will read, I kept my cool when later confronting its driver in the pit lane . . .

thought it was just pulling away from the right-hand barrier. There was just nothing I could do but brake hard. The Mirage went fish-tailing all over the place. I got so close to the 2-litre car that I could virtually read the serial number on its gearbox. I just managed to heave my way past on the outside, careering down the narrow grass verge separating the circuit from the guard rail. My heart was pounding, but I got away with it.

Cursing this guy, I went back to the pits and waited until this red 2-litre car eventually came into the pit lane. Then I advanced, obviously with a sufficiently menacing expression on my face to strike terror into this poor fellow in the cockpit. He just stayed there, strapped in, saying 'I'm sorry, I'm sorry . . .'

Fortunately, I paused before I said anything. That's right, it turned out to be the Gulf man's son. I just tried to show an almost paternal concern and slunk away tactfully, my point obviously made. That was one part of the endurance racing technique that I had to learn for myself. On the spot!

Chapter 6

Frankly speaking

ONE OF the better points about having been around the sport for a long time is the way one develops a personal perspective of its problems, shortcomings and plus points. In that respect, I am better placed than most to appreciate the enormous strides forward, the positive developments, that have been made in some areas, as well as other more negative aspects.

If I look back over the last 20 years it is gratifying to recall that motor racing safety has improved almost beyond recognition. When you are an up-and-coming driver, you are not really aware of the means by which the sport is operated and governed. You are too busy with your head down, trying to carve out a niche and a reputation for yourself. However, the very reason that I have survived to become an old and experienced professional racing driver is that there has been an opportunity for driver input on the question of motor racing safety. Moreover, by appealing for more developments on the safety front, as well as protecting our own skins, we have an opportunity to ensure a safer future for the next generation of aspiring stars, of which my son Justin happens to be one.

When my international racing career got off the ground, racing drivers were killed quite regularly. As I've already said, it was something which used to make quite a profound impression on me, but I'm not certain I really ever thought things would be different. My initial reaction, as you've read, was to question whether I was really suited for the sport. Happily, when we assess how things have developed, nobody can deny that motor racing is a great deal safer than it was when I embarked on that first Formula 2 season in 1968. We have safer cars to drive and, by and large, the circuit owners have done a very good job in improving their facilities and safety standards.

However, one point needs to be made very firmly. I remember reading in one of the English motor racing magazines last year some comments about driver attitudes towards safety developments at Le Mans. I detected the very firm implication that perhaps some of the older drivers were going soft, getting a bit past it. So let me make one very specific point. If the drivers have played any part in pressing for better safety at race tracks over the years, the real influence has been brought to bear by the more experienced men. We should never forget that.

Not by Nelson Piquet, we'll say, in his first season of Formula 3, but by Jackie Stewart in his *last* season of Formula 1. The experienced drivers have more clout because they can draw on more experience. So any critic who wants to get stuck into the senior drivers for 'going soft' ought to check their scripts very carefully and reflect on that at some length.

Taking a broader view, I have to say that I harbour misgivings about the management and administration of our sport at international level. I'm not talking about our own national sporting authority, the

Thumbs up from the scribes! Receiving my 1982 Driver of the Year award from Britain's Guild of Motoring Writers. I was extremely flattered when I was again elected to receive this award three years later.

RAC Motor Sports Association, because I don't have a great deal to do with it and, to be honest, as far as I'm concerned it does a fine job. Having said that, when I was out on the 1987 RAC Rally I talked to a lot of people involved in that area of the sport who felt that perhaps there was a lack of communication between the national authority and those taking part at grass roots level. However, the RAC MSA has been undergoing some reorganization and re-thinking over the past year or two, so things may well be changing on this front.

Over the years FISA has not really affected me too much, but as I've grown older I've felt that there is nobody at international level I can take my troubles to. If I have a gripe about anything to do with my IMSA racing programme in the USA, I can get hold of John Bishop and talk it through quite sensibly, informally, without a great deal of fuss. But it seems to me that there is nobody one can contact, as a sports car driver, who has a diplomatic feel for the problems. It is always easy to get one's own difficulties out of proportion, but I have the abiding feeling that the system of government in motor racing lacks the fine, sensitive touch. The system is arbitrary and too overtly uncompromising.

As an example, I remember an incident at the Nurburgring in 1986. Practice for the 1,000 km race had been stopped after one of the Jaguars spun off at a point where I was sitting in the pits at the wheel of my Rothmans Porsche having some minor adjustments carried out. When the damaged Jaguar was hauled past me along the pit lane, I followed it up to the pit exit where I stopped, intending to be first out on the circuit when practice resumed.

Unfortunately it appeared there would be a further delay to the schedule, so my crew called me up on the radio, saying, 'Derek, there's another ten minute wait before the track reopens, so you'd better come back to the pit'. At that point there was a tap on the window from one of the mechanics and he began pushing me backwards down the pit lane.

It was a fair old distance for him to have to push—between 80 and 100 yards—so I just tapped the PDK gearbox into reverse and gently shuffled back to my allotted place. All the time, the mechanic had his hand virtually resting on the Porsche, guiding me along at little more than walking pace. Ten minutes later the session was restarted and off I went.

At the end of the day I was dragged off to the stewards' office where the conversation went a bit like this. 'Mr Derek Bell?' 'Yes.' 'You are the World Champion?' 'Yes.' 'Well, we expect a driver in your position to know the rules. Do you deny that you reversed down the pit lane?' I replied that I didn't deny it, but as far as I was concerned practice was over for the time being. So they informed me, 'Ah no, you see the rules say that even when the programme is interrupted by an unscheduled delay, practice is still deemed to be taking place as far as these rules are concerned'. I thought this was splitting hairs, doing things by the book in true Germanic fashion. But

I tried to be helpful and respectful to them.

I explained that, in fact, the mechanic had been pushing me back, but that I had tapped the gear lever into reverse just to help him. Anyway, they all went off to deliberate in another room, leaving me to twiddle my thumbs for 20 minutes or so. They then called me in to tell me that they were fining me 1,000 deutschmarks.

I had been racing internationally for 20 years and this was the first time I had been up in front of the stewards.

To be honest, when I walked out of that meeting I was absolutely livid. I had been racing internationally for 20 years and this was the first time I had been up in front of the stewards. All right, I accept that I had committed an offence and that I should have been fully conversant with the rules, but under those circumstances, where there was an element of ambiguity about what had happened, I don't see why they could not have let me off with a formal warning. The way in which the whole decision was presented left me with the firm impression that they were just throwing their weight around for the sake of it. They were only interested in asserting their authority instead of taking what might be described as a constructive and conciliatory attitude. I felt I had been treated like a teenager, not like one of sports car racing's leading ambassadors.

I find it worrying that many of the people involved in motor racing's administration are often small-time politicians who have not, in my view, worked their way up through the ranks. Too many of them are not of motor racing, with a feel and a genuine concern for the sport. They are professional administrators who lack the gentle touch, and I feel very strongly that they do not always have the interests of the sport at the forefront of their minds.

I know people will think, 'Oh yes, this is just Bell letting off steam,' but I think those stewards at the Nurburgring could have shown themselves to be much more magnanimous. If they had taken the attitude, 'OK, let's give the guy a warning,' human nature being what it is, it would have had a much greater effect on me than having to pay a fine. I would have felt guilty, conscious that I had been let off lightly. It would have been a case of 'point taken' rather than getting my back up. They demonstrated this lack of feel for the situation which I referred to earlier on.

I'll give you another example of this arbitrary justice. At Jerez in 1987, Eddie Cheever was fined $10,000 for failing to sign on at race control prior to the start of practice. I don't care what viewpoint you hold, that penalty was *absolutely ludicrous*! It was another example, to my mind, of officials throwing their weight around just for the hell of it. What sort of response do they expect from the competitors under those circumstances? The whole episode just makes me livid if I so much as think about it.

If those officials had said, 'Look, Mr Cheever, we're sorry, but you really can't practise until you have signed on,' the whole situation would have been defused with the minimum of aggravation and tension. It's not as if Eddie had been throwing his weight around as the great prima donna American racing driver. That's not his style at all.

By the time we got to the drivers' meeting on race morning I was absolutely seething, determined that I would stand up and tell them that I thought the whole affair was an absolute disgrace. I regret that I didn't. Old Stucky was getting really concerned about how het-up I was, tugging my arm and whispering, 'For goodness sake, Derek, don't say that to them or we'll probably end up finding ourselves black-flagged during the race'. So I did allow myself to be intimidated into silence, which was wrong of me, but I think it provides an indication of how inhibited one feels in such situations.

Here's yet another example. At one race the stewards informed us, 'If you ignore the light signals at the end of the pit lane, we will call you in and tick you off'. Then somebody said, 'And what happens if it's the last lap of the race?' They instantly replied, 'In that case we'll fine you'. There seemed to be no thought about their response. It was just a knee-jerk reaction, an instant response. As if they plucked an idea out of the air.

I would love to work with FISA in some capacity to help the sport after my retirement.

I have always wanted to believe that everybody in motor racing fostered a great concern for the sport and its future. Frankly, I would love to work with FISA in some capacity to help the sport after my retirement from the cockpit, but not as long as they retain the arbitrary and dictatorial attitude which seems to prevail at the present time. Maybe there are people who will read this and say, 'Well, instead of being so critical, why doesn't Derek Bell make a more positive contribution to the sport?' All right, I take the point, but as I've already said *who* do I deal with at international level? Who is there to collaborate with? Who wants to know what I and the other drivers really think?

On a more positive note, I have enjoyed my time with the British Racing Drivers Club at Silverstone, which I hope has been quite constructive, and my relatively short time on the board of Brands Hatch Leisure. I can't offer them very much time while I'm still actively racing, but I hope that whatever input I can contribute will assist in short-cutting some of the inevitable difficulties which circuit

Receiving my Gold Star award from the British Racing Drivers Club in 1984, in the exalted company of Stirling Moss, Niki Lauda and Alain Prost. The BRDC's Gerald Lascelles looks on from the right.

owners face in their efforts to keep their tracks up to scratch. For example, if a suggestion comes up, I'm often in a position to say something like, 'Well, they tried that at Jarama and it didn't quite work. But if you do so-and-so, it might be better . . .' As the years pass, I'm desperately hoping I won't degenerate into the 'in my young days it was different' syndrome, even though the fact of the matter is I've been racing so long that I'm rather inclined to adopt it with my son Justin for some of the time. Anyway, I'm aware of that danger and I hope I always will be.

> We should never forget that we are purely professional entertainers.

Overall, though, I think it is a shame that more driver input is not used in shaping the sport's future because, as things stand at the moment, I believe that a relatively small handful of people are responsible for shaping motor racing's destiny. In my view we should never forget that we are purely professional entertainers, whether performing for the crowds in the grandstand or those who are watching on television. I am sure that Bernie Ecclestone would say he has this very point in mind when advancing the cause of the new silhouette saloon category which is due to be implemented in 1989 or 1990, but I am not certain I agree with him. We had a silhouette racing category in the late 1970s and it was very poorly supported. But maybe he is right inasmuch as we need to take a long-term view of the sport and restructure things slightly.

You might have Formula 3 on a Wednesday, Formula 3000 on Thursday, sports cars on Friday and Formula 1 on Saturday.

I made this fleeting single-seater comeback in Australia during 1978, driving Alan Hamilton's F5000 Lola-Chevy at Oran Park.

Perhaps there is even a case for promoting a packaged speed week concept which could be sold round the world as a festival of motor racing, rather like the major international athletics meetings, or Wimbledon fortnight. In Europe, for example, you might have Formula 3 on a Wednesday, Formula 3000 on Thursday, sports cars on Friday and Formula 1 on Saturday. The whole concept might make an excellent televised motorsports package. The circuits might well object, saying that nobody would turn up to spectate on the weekdays, but Wimbledon never has any problems attracting a crowd. And major athletics gatherings don't have the pole vault one weekend and the long jump the following weekend. The whole thing

Yes, I suppose you could say that I'm envious of those that got themselves better organized and made more of their Formula 1 opportunities. Here I am, perhaps rubbing salt into my own wounds, shaking down James Hunt's new ground-effect Wolf at Donington Park prior to the start of the 1979 Grand Prix season.

is shaped into one wide-ranging programme. It could be worth thinking about in a motor racing application.

Of course, one problem one would always be up against is the pre-eminent position of Formula 1. Grand Prix racing has always been the ultimate goal of every aspiring driver. I wanted to get there, and I'm sure that Justin and Jackie Stewart's son Paul will also want to make it into what, after all, has always been the number one category.

But there is room for all the top international categories. Perhaps sports car racing attracts a more knowledgeable crowd of specialized enthusiasts rather than the casual-interest spectator—aside from Le Mans, of course, which comes under the heading of a 'happening' rather like Wimbledon and the Indy 500, for example. Of course, because F1 is the leading category in the first place and has benefitted enormously from Bernie Ecclestone's entrepreneurial flair, it has now become probably the biggest sport in the world, leaving its contemporaries struggling to keep up.

There is no doubt that Bernie has done a fantastic job for Formula 1, but what concerns me is the way that his role has widened since he has become a FISA Vice-President. Sports car racing could benefit from the application of Bernie's business flair, though it also needs a sympathetic touch. It's not in the most healthy state, but it's a lot stronger than it has been at any time since the beginning of the 1970s, with Porsche, Jaguar and Mercedes all actively involved.

I suppose, if I am honest with myself, the future long-term development of international motor racing is unlikely to concern me as a driver for many more seasons. I will, obviously, be turning my thoughts to retirement before too long. But I have such a passionate

Top-class front row for the lawnmower race! From left to right: DB, Peter Gethin, Stirling Moss and David Purley. These could become pretty hectic affairs, which left participants bruised and battered for several days after.

enthusiasm for driving anything and everything anywhere it's offered, that life may seem a little on the dull side if I don't.

Away from the professional business of winning Group C races, I've derived an enormous amount of enjoyment from several off-beat activities, including such diverse attractions as lawnmower racing and trail biking, not to mention my Porsche driving school which has just got off the ground in the USA and which I'm developing as a potential retirement project! Al Holbert calls it 'The Derek Bell Annuity'.

The lawnmower racing business developed down here in Sussex as a charity fund-raising fun event at Wisborough Green in the mid-1970s and quickly attracted an enormous degree of interest. Its appeal has even spread as far as Australia where I've found myself being interviewed more about my lawnmower racing exploits than my outings for Porsche! The Wisborough Green event was initiated as a 12-hour affair, starting when the pubs closed on Saturday night and running through to opening time on the Sunday morning. All in all, a most civilized business!

All sorts of celebrities have been involved, from Oliver Reed to Stirling Moss, and the whole business has proved to be enormous fun! There are three classes, the top runners being four-wheelers with twin rear tyres, some with such luxuries as Recaro seats. Then there are the original roller types, with the box on the front and a tractor seat—the original racing concept, so to speak—and finally the smaller class 'driven' by teams who take turns in running along behind. The local rugby or athletics clubs turn out to field teams in this latter class, running for five laps at a time, and it can all be pretty lurid during the night, when your spotlights are broken, lurching about over the bumps when you come up to one of these guys running for all they are worth behind their mower. By the time we finish the race, we're all suffering from the most appalling bruising and muscular strain because the track usually dries out to the point where it's rather like motor racing across a cattle grid.

Continuing my theme of messing about with machinery, I got involved in enduro riding in the late 1970s. I won an 80 cc Kawasaki, which initially Justin used for nipping round the paddocks at British race meetings. Then my old friend John Penfold, with whom I started my career racing a Lotus Seven back in 1964, got his hands on a 175 cc Yamaha trail bike and we used to mess around up at the local gravel quarry, having one hell of a good time. Justin and John's son James also got involved and I later moved up via a 250 cc Suzuki to a 400 cc Husqvarna which was just so much pure fun you can hardly begin to believe!

Enduro riding is an unbelievable challenge which I found absolutely intoxicating. I really got the taste of it with several events throughout the country, highlighted by the Welsh International Two Day Trial, a couple of spectacular 100-mile laps round the Brecon Beacons area which I did with John Penfold plus David Purley, just after he had recuperated from that dreadful British Grand Prix practice shunt which effectively ended his racing career in 1977. My wife Pam used to refer to the three of us as 'Last of the Summer Wine!' It really was such a terrific challenge. We made it a real family affair with everybody going up and Justin and James Penfold competing against their fathers, both of them well able to, I may say, because by now they were also competing in schoolboy motocross events all over the south of England.

I derived enormous pleasure from preparing and working on my own bike after all those years of having other people preparing the racing cars I drove in a professional capacity. The top aces in this very specialized form of motor cycling are just *so* talented, but it is really a big commercial business like pure circuit racing, and they don't make much money or receive due acknowledgement for their terrific skill.

For getting really fit, I don't think I've ever experienced anything quite like it.

This enduro-biking is one of the few sports in which a relative novice can get out on the same event as a really top exponent and pit his skill against the best in the business. The exhilaration of hurtling across grass-covered hillsides at between 70 and 80 mph, all alone, balancing on the back wheel for much of the time as you leap from bump to bump, is just something that has to be experienced to be believed. It's one of those things which is purely down to your own skill; there's nobody else to blame if you go wrong and make a

Opposite *Enduro-biking afforded both Justin and I a tremendous amount of exhilaration. It is just the rider and his bike against the wild terrain, with nobody else intervening to help, hinder or compromise one's chances!*

Below *Trying a Honda for size – suitably dressed, I might add. But it was only a 'roadie', not the full racing kit!*

mistake, just as there isn't a pit crew moaning at you about your lap times or a co-driver shouting details of the next corner. If I bounced on my own head, then it was nobody's fault but my own. If I broke the bike, then I just loaded it back on to the trailer and drove off home. If I managed to finish without hurting myself I was really elated. For getting really fit, I don't think I've ever experienced anything quite like it.

In addition, it gave me the great pleasure of competing with Justin in the same event, although I will admit that it could get rather worrying at times. I remember on one occasion finishing a stage only to be asked, 'Have you got a shovel with you?' 'Why?' I inquired. Back came the response, 'Because I've just passed your son sitting up to his waist in a bog. Somebody will need to get out and rescue him!' So then it was a case of climbing into the old Range Rover and trying to find my way round to where he was stranded. Sure enough, there he was, up to his waist in this glutinous mud, with only one of the bike's handlebars still in sight. He didn't have the strength to pull the bike out by himself, so it was Dad who had to get his boots filled with mud to salvage the equipment.

I haven't done any of these enduro events for the last two years, but I can still vividly recall the challenge of it all. And what made it even nicer was the fact that the people involved in it were extremely warm and hospitable, ready to dispense advice freely to newcomers, as well as having a splendid sense of humour. Caked with mud, freezing cold, bruised and battered, lost in the middle of nowhere, a sense of humour was probably something of an asset!

More recently, I got involved in rallying in time to take part in the 1987 RAC Rally. It was an area of the sport that I had always had in the back of my mind to have a crack at, but pressures from my racing career and other business interests had always conspired against me. I have to confess that I had never been very keen to take part in small events round the Sussex lanes, concentrating on map reading and suchlike, but over the years I grew to know people such as Roger Clark, Ari Vatanen and Henri Toivonen. In addition, Jacky Ickx was always saying, 'Why don't you have a try at the Paris-Dakar?' which he actually won. But while I really wanted to take part, there was obviously no way the factory was about to install me in a turbo four-wheel-drive Porsche rally car without me having some experience in another, similar event. Just before Christmas, 1987, I met Jean-Pierre Jarier at a skiing weekend in Switzerland and he said to me, 'Derek, I just can't think why you're not doing the Paris-Dakar in the New Year. A group of us are doing it in Range Rovers; you ought to be out there, with British backing, at the wheel of another one!'

It sounded all good, enthusiastic stuff and it is still an event I would dearly love to participate in. The trouble is, of course, that the pressures on my time are simply enormous and, as things stand at the moment, it would be almost impossible to fit such an event into my schedule. None the less, the Paris-Dakar, for all the tragic

Off-track fun with the 'Driving Force' team. Group photo including myself and Barry Lee, Anneka Rice, Nigel Mansell, Murray Walker, Malcolm MacDonald, Tony Pond and Rowan Atkinson.

accidents that befell competitors in the 1988 event, remains a tantalizing adventure that I find myself extremely attracted to.

My participation in the RAC Rally served only to sharpen my appetite for more similar outings. It was at the 1987 Brands Hatch 1,000 km sports car race that Paul Davies, PR for Rothmans, first casually asked me whether I would be interested in doing the rally. I replied, 'Great. Very much indeed!' and I thought it would never go any further. Then, out of the blue, came an offer from General Motors. Would I like to drive an Astra in the Group A class of the rally? It would be a works-supported car, but it would be necessary for me to raise some sponsorship to run it. So my business manager David Mills got on to some of my own personal sponsors, asking whether they would be interested in such a project. Unfortunately there were no takers, so I was inclined to forget the whole project and concentrate my efforts on sorting out my racing programme for 1988.

Finally, while I was in America during September, there was a telephone call from David to say that GM were underwriting the whole cost of the programme and if we could raise any personal sponsorship then that could be regarded as my driving fee. I was delighted that we were in business together!

In order to get some idea of the rally driving technique at close quarters, I went up to the Gaydon test track for some tuition from Malcolm Wilson, front runner in the GM rally line-up. He'd been testing regularly on that special stage for about four years, so I have to confess I found the whole thing a bit of an eye-opener.

After a couple of laps storming down these rutted tracks, I was putting a brave face on it all, trying to be as casual and relaxed as I possibly could. Inwardly I was thinking, 'What on earth has Mills got me involved in? I quite understand why people have told me I shouldn't be doing it. This is crazy. Total lunacy!' Eventually, though, I came round to the opinion that Malcolm didn't want to die either, but I did make a firm note to myself that it really wasn't quite as funny a business as it may have looked at first sight!

Realistically, I really knew that it was going to be one of the biggest challenges of my career, although the casual 'oh, you'll-love-the-whole-thing-and-do-well!' attitude which prevailed amongst many of my colleagues had clearly started to rub off on me. I began to think about how people must feel when they ride 'shotgun' with me in one of the works Porsche sports cars and, by the end of the session, I was yelling 'Yes, go on Malcolm, let's have another lap!' Inwardly, I felt scared stiff . . .

Then it was my turn to have a stint behind the wheel. I did three or four laps of the track and loved every second of it. I could have gone on, non-stop, all day. It was my first time on the loose—apart from with the lawnmowers!—my first time trying left-foot braking and with front-wheel drive. Furthermore, it was great to be working with such a competitive team which gave me so much support and helped enormously with my confidence.

It felt very strange relying on another person to provide me with details of the road ahead.

And so we went into the event, co-driver Mike Nicholson strapped in alongside me, trying to look relaxed and fairly nonchalant about the whole situation. That was the first thing I found so strange and unfamiliar, of course; taking advice from somebody sitting alongside me. After all those years as a racing driver making my own split-second decisions, it felt very strange indeed suddenly to find myself in a situation where I was relying on another person to provide me with details of the road ahead.

In addition, I found it difficult to remember rally lingo for the various corners. 'Fast K,' 'Slow K,' '90-right' . . . it was a case of improvising all the time and making constant references to the check list which I had taped to the centre console. It was terrific fun, but didn't last too long as just about anybody who followed the event will know all too well. My embarrassment at being stranded in one of the water splashes was graphically relayed nationwide on television. The engine filled up with water and we eventually retired with a bent connecting rod.

I had been through an earlier water splash—prior to the televised one—and flooded the engine. I naturally assumed we had just

Using identical Chevy Camaros, the IROC series brings together a selection of driving talent from a wide variety of different racing categories. Here I am running in close company with Tom Sneva and my Porsche colleague Jochen Mass on the banking at Michigan International Speedway in 1985.

swamped the electrics, but thankfully it started on the button again once the marshals helped push us out. At the televised water splash I eased back to a crawl, but the engine just stopped dead the moment we entered the water. What had happened was that the engine air intake, ducted through the front spoiler, had just steered water straight into the cylinders. The pistons were now trying to push against a couple of litres of water and, of course, it was no contest.

The marshals were simply incredible. They just attacked the engines with cans of WD40, but by this time the damage had been done and the con-rod was obviously bent. On the next special stage I began to relax and get into the rhythm of things when the engine started to misfire owing to a faulty potentiometer in the fuel injection system, which was changed and then ran perfectly through to the middle of the day before blowing up on our return to Oulton Park. Shortly afterwards, we were out.

To be honest, I felt a little bit uncomfortable about all the publicity which surrounded me, particularly when I heard one onlooker say, 'You're going to win, aren't you?' It made me slightly uneasy but, as somebody made the point, I was probably the best-known English driver in the rally. It was a great shame I didn't get further into the event. Although Mike Nicholson may have thought otherwise on the strength of those first few stages, I was trying to adopt the long-distance racing approach, attempting to conserve the machinery. Mike was shouting, 'All right, all right . . . if you don't try so hard, you'll go faster . . .' and I was shouting, 'but it's fun, isn't it?' When he said he agreed with that last remark, I must admit I wasn't totally convinced.

One way or another, it wasn't a terribly good rally for the GM team and the crew was generally pretty depressed once it was over. We all went into a bar for a drink after cleaning up and I noticed a jazz group playing in one corner of the lounge. There was nothing else for it but to borrow their trumpet player, walk him out to where the GM crew was waiting and play 'The Last Post' in front of a crowd of sponsors, journalists, PR men and other supporters!

I like to think that loosened everybody up after what had been a pretty disappointing day, but team manager Melvin Hodgson, who was within this group, had already asked me whether I would do the RAC with them next year the moment I climbed out of the car. I just replied, 'You bet your life I will!'

Planning for the future: the cover of a brochure for the Porsche Precision Driving School with Derek Bell, which has taken off with such promising effect in the USA.

PRECISION DRIVING SCHOOL
WITH DEREK BELL

PORSCHE

I can't begin to pretend that I'm likely to have an unlimited future as a rally driver.

Having said all that, I can't begin to pretend that I'm likely to have an unlimited future as a rally driver. As far as long-term business involvements are concerned, the Porsche School of Precision Driving with Derek Bell, which I started in the USA towards the end of 1987, is a project which could really represent a major slice of my post-retirement plans.

The idea behind it stemmed from the 'customer track days' which I used to set up for BMW in the UK. It was a tremendously successful method of promoting and selling their range. BMW would supply up to 25 cars which would be handled by professional racing drivers. Prospective customers would be invited to ride round with these drivers for a demonstration of the car's finer points. It worked extremely well and whetted my appetite to start my own operation. Later I did some similar customer days for Porsche in the UK, all of which seemed to produce a very favourable reaction.

Eventually, I was approached by Ken Fengler, President of the Florida Gold Coast region of the Porsche Owners' Club, to host a driving weekend at Moroso Raceway in West Palm Beach. They all loved it and it wasn't long before I found myself inundated with offers. 'Can you come up to Connecticut and do a day here? Can you go somewhere else and do a day there?' And so it went on. Ken and I came to the conclusion that there was a natural market for this sort of project. We did a couple more Derek Bell days at Moroso and they seemed to go very well. So we took it from there.

I knew full well that Peter Schutz wanted a Porsche driving school in the USA, so Porsche USA asked us to send a proposition as to precisely what we had in mind. At the same time they sent us their ideas and, happily, they were pretty well identical and we quickly finalized an arrangement.

The whole thing basically revolves round a group of invited Porsche owners bringing their own cars for specialized tuition at various race circuits on the Tuesday after an IMSA sports car race. The whole package includes tickets to the race, then on the Monday night we hold a cocktail party and dinner and I give them a little chat about what we're going to do the following day. I like to get all the nitty gritty out of the way before they get to the track so that they can get the maximum enjoyment, and time out on the circuit, for their money.

Basically, we concentrate on smooth driving techniques, helping owners to get the best out of their high-performance machines with as much safety and security as possible. We have a maximum of around 30 people, start at 8.30 in the morning and, up to lunchtime, concentrate on various specific exercises which will brush up their style. In the afternoon they are allowed to get out and do some serious lapping on the circuit. We find that people don't want to lap for hours, probably because we're not catering for people who want to be racing drivers. We're aiming at people keen to understand their Porsche's potential more than they do and get an accurate bearing on their own ability. I guarantee, almost without fail, that they go home at the end of the day driving better than they did when they arrived.

Sometimes you can also help people. One gentleman who turned up with a 930 Turbo was really quite nervous and, by the end of the day, had managed to spin off the road. I discussed his performance with him and it turned out that he was an eye specialist who spent most of his working day wound up with intense concentration. 'At the end of the day, I want a car that is soothing and relaxing to drive on my way home,' he explained. 'This 930 keeps me concentrating, on the edge of my seat, just as intensely as I have to in the surgery.' I suggested the answer might be swapping to a 928S!

At the end of the course we always send out a questionnaire asking all the owners why they attended the school. The best answer of all was, 'Because I've got a Porsche 930 and don't want to die!'

Above all, I want the course to be fun for the participants. Customers should not go away with the impression that they have been ordered around in a schoolmasterly fashion. I always make this point to the instructors. We want them to enjoy themselves in a relaxed atmosphere which also helps them to produce their best. The Americans tend to respond extremely well to this sort of operation. They really like getting involved and seem to appreciate our efforts to ensure that they have a worthwhile day out in a friendly, responsible environment.

The remaining, extremely important, area that I want to reflect on from a personal point of view is the way in which my family life has been obliged to adapt itself round my motor racing. Pam and I have known each other since before I started my first motor race in the Lotus Seven I shared with John Penfold. The daughter of a vet from Ashby-de-la-Zouch, in Leicestershire, she was starting out on a career as a model when we met up for the first time in 1962. Our first date was at the Smithfield Show in London where, as I recall, we didn't kick off on too clever a note because we spent an hour or so each waiting for the other at different entrances!

For five years we went out together, on and off, with me going through the inevitable spells when I wanted to marry her and she didn't want to marry me, and vice versa; the sort of indecision that many young couples go through. Finally, in 1967 we were married. Justin was born in 1968, followed by Melanie in 1969.

From a pure career point of view, a young racing driver doesn't really need to be married. The whole business is rather a selfish situation and you tend to find yourself being pulled in opposite directions. Basically one *wants* to be married. It seems the natural course of events, although whether it's exactly what you *require* as a young racer is another matter altogether.

It's not been easy, although as Pam and I surveyed the scene at the end of 1987 we decided that perhaps we hadn't done too badly when we look around to see how many of our contemporaries are still married to the same person as they were 20 years ago. I'm really grateful to her for doing such a great job bringing up the children when I haven't been around nearly as much as she would have liked me to be.

I'm afraid the whole situation boils down to one basic fact. Anybody who is going to be really successful in this life is probably not going to

Family, 1968; Pam with me in the pits at Monza prior to my outing for Ferrari in the Italian Grand Prix.

do it by working a regular nine-to-five job and, most likely, will find themselves being obliged to spend time away from their family on business. So it is not a lifestyle which leads to an easy relationship. I suppose it's possible to argue that we have been together longer than a lot of people because we *have* been apart, because we are not making life claustrophobic by being on top of each other all the time.

Another point, of course, is that, if you were a bank manager, you wouldn't take your wife to the office, would you? So why would you want to take her to a motor race if you are a racing driver? Of course, the most immediate difference is obviously the fact that, as a racing driver, you don't always come home that same night and when you are commuting round the world all the time tensions do tend to build up.

The more successful you become, the more you tend to be away, so the whole thing develops into a vicious circle. We all want to be successful, deep down inside. Nobody in their right mind is going to say, 'I'm sorry, that's enough. I don't want to be any more successful than this. I've got to stop. I don't want to earn any more money.' Once you get the taste of earning decent money, you want to earn more of it. And, make no mistake, money becomes no more easier to earn the more successful you become.

How team managers and mechanics come to terms with all these pressures I just cannot begin to understand.

How team managers and mechanics come to terms with all these pressures I just cannot begin to understand. At least when I get home I can spend some time with my family, but to come off the plane and then be obliged to head straight back to the factory and get on with the job of preparing the cars must be an absolute nightmare. I don't understand how they cope with all that. I guess under those circumstances you've just got to have a very special wife indeed.

To be honest, Pam has never been terribly interested in my motor racing. Sometimes I think that in itself has been quite beneficial, yet on other occasions I find myself wishing she had enjoyed it more. On the other hand, in practical terms, it's a bit difficult to see how a wife can be involved in the day-to-day business of motor racing. Generally, I don't believe ladies do find a lot to interest themselves, long-term, in the sport. They may show considerable interest for a time, but eventually they feel, 'Oh, I'm sick of this . . .' because it's so intense and blinkered that, unless you are deeply involved in it, you don't want to know. Sadly, of such problems are broken marriages made.

As I say, I think she's done a great job bringing up the children. I

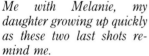

Me with Melanie, my daughter growing up quickly as these two last shots remind me.

know I'm bound to be biased, but I think I've two amazingly good kids and we're tremendously close. We really are terrifically fond of each other. When I consider Melanie is a grown woman and Justin almost into his twenties, when I meet either of them at the airport I still kiss them both and give them a big hug which I think reflects the fact that we've kept a really close personal relationship. That delights me.

Now, what is the reason behind this? Is it because I've been away a lot while they were growing up? Is it a basically good family environment in which they've been brought up? Is it that they like both having me away and seeing me come home? I really don't know. Perhaps if I'd been at home all the time there might have been more friction. As it is, Justin loves living at home at a time when he's saving every penny for his own racing programme. Melanie has flown the nest and is making a career for herself. She is fluent in French, following a spell working for Moet, and is a lovely looking girl who is doing very well for herself. Both she and Justin have hearts of gold and, although Justin is quite the untidiest person I have ever met in my life, I think they've both got delightful personalities and I love them dearly.

So, in real terms, I don't think motor racing has harmed us at all although, ironically, it has really only been Pam who has suffered in any way from my career. She's not only had the pressure of bringing up the children on her own for much of the time, but also her illness which was aggravated by worries over my racing. She's had a tough time because I've not been around when she's needed me. I suppose it's easy to say that I could have been a lot more successful in my fledgling days with Ferrari had I not been married, or had Pam not been ill. But, that said, such considerations wouldn't have stopped me getting married because that's what I wanted to do and I have certainly never regretted it. I'm very satisfied with what's happened in my motor racing and personal life.

In material terms, we've benefitted enormously, of course. All of us. We've got a lovely home. We've had super holidays all round the world, been invited as guests to exciting places like Dubai, been entertained in some of the best skiing resorts in Europe. All that has been a direct by-product, a spin-off from my motor racing. The sport has been very kind to us all, but that doesn't alter the fact that Pam doesn't like motor racing at the end of the day. Nothing is going to change that reality.

I hope I've never taken things for granted. I've appreciated and been grateful for the things my family have had from motor racing. I've enjoyed it immensely. All that terrifies me now is the fact that, touch wood, to date I've been exceptionally lucky and never really hurt myself seriously. I just pray that Justin will get through his racing career with as much good fortune as I've enjoyed. From Pam's point of view, the prospect of another 20 years of a second member of the family being absorbed in motor racing is not exactly something she relishes. A real case of 'here we go again . . .'

I don't know how one reconciles the pressures produced by a motor racing marriage. All these material benefits, at the end of the day, don't really compensate the family for the fact that one is away from home for a long time. Pam would probably rather have had me home, doing the normal things that normal families do. Yet I don't believe I could ever be a stereotyped nine-to-five merchant.

Anyway, having a family and a firm base down here in Sussex has given me an enormous feeling of stability and security throughout my racing career. I remember particularly during the pressure of those early Ferrari days, trying to get a foot on the Formula 1 ladder, the sheer relaxation and sense of relief to drive down that avenue of trees to the cottage where we lived in those days, just up the lane from our present home. I'm certain that the fact that I've always lived down here in Pagham throughout my racing career, close to the rest of my family, spending my spare time with the same friends that I knocked about with 25 years ago, has helped me keep my feet firmly on the ground. It's terrific jetting all over the world, but it's even better to know, in the back of your mind all the time, that there is that familiar, comfortable home base to return to.

Coming down from London, clearing the South Downs near Petworth, from where you can almost see the English Channel on a sunny day, I suddenly feel more relaxed and carefree. I never had the urge to live anywhere else, certainly not jostling around in London. I might have enjoyed it for a short time had I been single, but my roots are down here in Sussex. I can't imagine living anywhere else.

As for what will replace motor racing when I finally stop, I just don't know. I can't see myself racing for much longer, yet, on the other hand, since I've been involved in the US scene I see people like Mario Andretti, Al Unser Senior and the other CART boys, all older than me, all doing extremely well in a much more competitive class than I am. What's more, whenever I mention to some of my American friends that I might be retiring in the next couple of years, they just look at me in disbelief and say, 'What do you mean? You can't stop yet. Not at your age!'

In many ways, this highlights a fundamental difference between motor racing in America and over here in Britain. In the USA motor racing is a total way of life. Here, being a professional sportsman is almost something you do if you can't make your mark as a lawyer or an accountant. In some ways, being a sportsman is still rather frowned on in some quarters. It's better than it used to be, I accept, but you still get the feeling that some people rather disapprove of the whole thing.

I'm sure some people look at Justin in that sort of light. 'Oh look at him, he's very lucky . . .' That sort of approach. But there he is, with

Second generation Bell. My son Justin in the cockpit of the Ray Formula Ford single-seater he raced throughout 1987. Here I am looking in mock incredulity at his lap times during a test session at Goodwood. I pray he has as safe a motor racing career as I have been lucky enough to experience.

Above *Great day: with the family outside Buckingham Palace in 1987 after the presentation of my MBE for services to motor racing.*

Right *Family, 1987; Justin, Pam, me and Melanie on the lawn at Little Welbourne. It doesn't seem like 19 years . . .*

Back on Church Farm. I still take an active interest, although the tractors tend to be a lot bigger than when I used to mess around as a child in the early 1950s!

the opportunity to make a great career out of motor racing if he has the talent. But people say, 'Oh, he's had it on a plate'. In America, there was never any doubt that the young Andrettis and Unsers would go motor racing and they had considerable assistance. Nobody moaned about that because the whole mood, the emphasis, is different over there. It's a question of good luck if you find yourself in a fortunate position.

Of course, if Justin hasn't got the talent, there is basically nothing I can do to help him, for all my experience. I have been able to assist him by short-cutting some of the problems which inevitably face novice racing drivers. Although I went to the Jim Russell Racing School in my early years, I took Justin out of racing school quite early on because I figured there was nothing that I couldn't teach him, assuming he has the basic talent. A racing school is good for giving people a chance of getting into a racing car when they otherwise might not have had the opportunity. But it won't help you make the grade if you haven't the talent.

When the time comes, I hope I will be able to stop sensibly and not make a bloody idiot of myself. This team of Justin's is going to be called Derek Bell Racing, so this could provide me with an interest which could continue over the years and be of benefit to my son. So, to sum it all up, I really don't know what I'm going to do when I retire from the cockpit. I would like to help with the sport, but I'm terrified of being labelled an 'old fogey' and part of the conservative motor racing establishment. That way you end up being absorbed into the system and become the sort of figure that I've been critical of in this chapter. I'm very anxious that I don't lose my feel for the day-to-day

How I would like to be remembered – still capable of winning. I just hope I'll know when is the right time to stop.

problems faced by an active racing driver.

That said, I can't imagine retiring from the cockpit, washing my hands of the whole motor racing business and walking away from the sport altogether, without a backward glance. It's been so much part of my life for 25 years—over half my life—that I'm too absorbed in it. Sure, I have regrets. I wish that I'd made the grade in Formula 1, perhaps catching Ferrari at a better time or benefitting from a season with Brabham in 1972. But I've never been bitter about it, merely envious of others who got their act together better than I did.

When the time comes, I hope I will be able to stop sensibly and not make a bloody idiot of myself.

I don't believe that when motor racing is taken out of my life I will be pounding around the place like a caged lion, looking for things to do. I still take an active part in the family business down here and, with my Porsche driving school in the USA, there is obviously potential for quite a rewarding business future.

But it will never be quite the same. I cannot conceive of anything which will quite produce such elation as the sport which has brought me so much over the best part of three decades. It has been kind to me and I've achieved a fair deal. More importantly, I've enjoyed pretty well every minute of it.

It would have been difficult to ask for more.

International racing record

Derek's career began on Saturday 13 March 1964 when he won his very first motor race at Goodwood driving the Lotus Seven he shared with close friend John Penfold. His international career began briefly in 1965 with a handful of outings in major F3 events with his Lotus 31, although national level club races were his main preoccupation. It was not until 1966, when he acquired his Lotus 41, that he embarked on a major programme of events in Europe. This record of his career embraces his international successes, although significant minor-league results on the British domestic scene have also been included.

1965	10 Jul	Silverstone	F3 Lotus 31	Rtd
	24 Jul	Silverstone	F3 Lotus 31	Rtd
	30 Aug	Brands Hatch	F3 Lotus 31	Rtd

1966	20 Mar	Goodwood	F3 Lotus 41	3rd
	17 Apr	Pau	F3 Lotus 41	Rtd
	24 Apr	Barcelona	F3 Lotus 41	Did not start
	14 May	Silverstone (GP)	F3 Lotus 41	6th
	21 May	Monaco	F3 Lotus 41	Did not qualify
	29 May	Chimay	F3 Lotus 41	9th
	30 May	Goodwood	F3 Lotus 41	2nd
	12 Jun	Goodwood	F3 Lotus 41	**1st**
	19 Jun	Caserta	F3 Lotus 41	Rtd
	10 Jul	Silverstone	F3 Lotus 41	Rtd
	24 Jul	Silverstone	F3 Lotus 41	Rtd
	7 Aug	Crystal Palace	F3 Lotus 41	5th
	28 Aug	Brands Hatch	F3 Lotus 41	Rtd
	18 Sept	Monza	F3 Lotus 41	Rtd

25 Sept	Albi	*F3 Lotus 41*	6th
2 Oct	Silverstone	*F3 Lotus 41*	3rd
26 Dec	Brands Hatch	*F3 Brabham BT21*	**1st**

1967

22 Jan	Brands Hatch	*F3 Brabham BT21*	**1st**
5 Mar	Snetterton	*F3 Brabham BT21*	**1st**
27 Mar	Silverstone	*F3 Brabham BT21*	4th
2 Apr	Pau	*F3 Brabham BT21*	5th
9 Apr	Barcelona	*F3 Brabham BT21*	2nd
29 Apr	Silverstone	*F3 Brabham BT21*	Rtd
6 May	Monaco	*F3 Brabham BT21*	3rd
14 May	Chimay	*F3 Brabham BT21*	3rd
20 May	Silverstone	*F3 Brabham BT21*	**1st**
29 May	Castle Combe	*F3 Brabham BT21*	**1st**
4 Jun	Djurslandring	*F3 Brabham BT21*	Rtd
18 Jun	Clermont Ferrand	*F3 Brabham BT21*	3rd
24 Jun	Reims	*F3 Brabham BT21*	Rtd
2 Jul	Le Mans (Bugatti)	*F3 Brabham BT21*	Rtd
15 Jul	Silverstone	*F3 Brabham BT21*	6th
29 Jul	Djurslandring	*F3 Brabham BT21*	Race stopped
5 Aug	Crystal Palace	*F3 Brabham BT21*	5th
13 Aug	Nogaro	*F3 Brabham BT21*	2nd
27 Aug	Ollon-Villars	*F3 Brabham BT21*	**1st in class**
9 Sept	Crystal Palace	*F3 Brabham BT21*	2nd
17 Sept	Zolder	*F3 Brabham BT21*	**1st**
24 Sept	Albi	*F3 Brabham BT21*	2nd
1 Oct	Hockenheim	*F3 Brabham BT21*	Rtd
21 Oct	Oulton Park	*F3 Brabham BT21*	**1st**

	29 Oct	Brands Hatch	*F3 Brabham BT21*	9th
	26 Dec	Brands Hatch	*F3 Brabham BT21*	2nd
1968	*31 Mar*	Barcelona	*F2 Brabham BT23C*	Did not start
	7 Apr	Hockenheim	*F2 Brabham BT23C*	Rtd
	15 Apr	Thruxton	*F2 Brabham BT23C*	3rd
	21 Apr	Nurburgring	*F2 Brabham BT23C*	3rd
	28 Apr	Jarama	*F2 Brabham BT23C*	Rtd
	5 May	Zolder	*F2 Brabham BT23C*	Rtd
	3 Jun	Crystal Palace	*F2 Brabham BT23C*	Rtd
	23 Jun	Monza Lottery	*F2 Ferrari 166*	Rtd
	14 Jul	Tulln-Langenlebarn	*F2 Ferrari 166*	7th
	28 Jul	Zandvoort	*F2 Ferrari 166*	14th
	17 Aug	Oulton Park	*F1 Ferrari 312*	Rtd
	25 Aug	Enna-Pergusa	*F2 Ferrari 166*	5th
	8 Sept	Italian Grand Prix	*F1 Ferrari 312*	Rtd
	6 Oct	US Grand Prix	*F1 Ferrari 312*	Rtd
	13 Oct	Hockenheim	*F2 Ferrari 166*	6th
	27 Oct	Vallelunga	*F2 Ferrari 166*	6th
1969	*4 Jan*	New Zealand Grand Prix	*Ferrari 246*	4th
	11 Jan	Levin	*Ferrari 246*	Rtd
	18 Jan	Christchurch	*Ferrari 246*	5th
	25 Jan	Teretonga Park	*Ferrari 246*	5th
	2 Feb	Australian GP, Lakeside	*Ferrari 246*	2nd
	9 Feb	Warwick Farm	*Ferrari 246*	2nd
	16 Feb	Sandown Park	*Ferrari 246*	5th
	30 Mar	Silverstone	*F1 Ferrari 312*	9th
	7 Apr	Thruxton	*F2 Ferrari 166*	Rtd
	27 Apr	Nurburgring	*F2 Ferrari 166*	5th
	11 May	Jarama	*F2 Ferrari 166*	8th
	22 May	Monza Lottery	*F2 Ferrari 166*	5th
	19 Jul	British GP, Silverstone	*McLaren M9A 4WD*	Rtd
	12 Oct	Vallelunga	*F2 Brabham BT30*	4th
1970	*4 Jan*	Levin	*F1 Brabham BT26A*	Rtd
	11 Jan	New Zealand Grand Prix	*F1 Brabham BT26A*	2nd

18 Jan	Christchurch	F1 Brabham BT26A	Rtd
30 Mar	Thruxton	F2 Brabham BT30	3rd
5 Apr	Pau	F2 Brabham BT30	4th
12 Apr	Hockenheim	F2 Brabham BT30	3rd
26 Apr	Barcelona	F2 Brabham BT30	**1st**
3 May	Nurburgring	F2 Brabham BT30	2nd
17 May	Spa 1,000 km	Ferrari 512M	4th (with Hughes de Fierlant)
24 May	Zolder	F2 Brabham BT30	2nd
25 May	Crystal Palace	F2 Brabham BT30	6th
7 Jun	Belgian Grand Prix	F3 Brabham BT26A	Rtd
13/14 Jun	Le Mans 24-hrs	Ferrari 512M	Rtd
2 Aug	Nurburgring	F2 Brabham BT30	Rtd
23 Aug	Enna-Pergusa	F2 Brabham BT30	Rtd
13 Sept	Tulln Langenlebarn	F2 Brabham BT30	4th
27 Sept	Imola	F2 Brabham BT30	3rd
4 Oct	US Grand Prix	F1 Surtees TS7	6th
11 Oct	Hockenheim	F2 Brabham BT30	6th
7 Nov	Kyalami 9-hrs	Ferrari 512M	4th

1971

10 Jan	Buenos Aires 1,000 km	Porsche 917	**1st** (with Jo Siffert)
24 Jan	Argentine Grand Prix	F1 March 701	Rtd
30-31 Jan	Daytona 24-hrs	Porsche 917	Rtd
7 Feb	Bogota	F2 March 712M	7th
14 Feb	Bogota	F1 March 712M	3rd
20 Mar	Sebring 12-hrs	Porsche 917	5th (with Jo Siffert)
28 Mar	Questor Grand Prix (US)	F1 March 701	Rtd
2 Apr	Brands Hatch 1,000 km	Porsche 917	3rd (with Jo Siffert)
12 Apr	Thruxton	F2 March 712M	3rd
25 Apr	Monza 1,000 km	Porsche 917	2nd (with Jo Siffert)
2 May	Nurburgring	F2 March 712M	Rtd
9 May	Spa 1,000 km	Porsche 917	2nd (with Jo Siffert)
30 May	Nurburgring 1,000 km	Porsche 908/3	Rtd
31 May	Crystal Palace	F2 March 712M	Rtd
12-13 Jun	Le Mans 24-hrs	Porsche 917	Rtd
27 Jun	Austrian 1,000 km	Porsche 917	Rtd
31 Jun	Monza Lottery	F2 March 712M	2nd
4 Jul	Hockenheim Interserie	McLaren M8E	**1st**

17 Jul	British GP, Silverstone	*Surtees TS9*	Rtd
24 Jul	Watkins Glen 6-hrs	*Porsche 917*	3rd (with Richard Attwood)
8 Aug	Mantorp Park	*F2 March 712M*	9th
30 Aug	Brands Hatch	*F2 March 712M*	Did not qualify
26 Sept	Albi	*F2 March 712M*	Did not qualify
10 Oct	Vallelunga	*F2 March 712M*	Rtd
12 Oct	Barcelona 1,000 km	*Porsche 917*	2nd (with Gijs van Lennep)
17 Oct	Paris 1,000 km	*Porsche 917*	**1st** (with Gijs van Lennep)

1972

6 Feb	Sebring 12-hrs	*Mirage M6*	Rtd
16 Apr	Brands Hatch 1,000 km	*Mirage M6*	Rtd
30 Apr	Nurburgring F2	*Brabham BT38*	2nd
7 May	Spa 1,000 km	*Mirage M6*	4th (with Gijs van Lennep)
28 May	Nurburgring 1,000 km	*Mirage M6*	Rtd
10-11 Jun	Le Mans 24-hrs	*Ferrari 365GTB*	8th (with Teddy Pilette and Richard Bond)
18 Jun	Watkins Glen	*F5000 McLaren M10B*	8th
25 Jun	Austrian 1,000 km	*Mirage M6*	Rtd
4 Jul	French Grand Prix	*F1 Tecno PA123*	Did not start
16 Jul	Road America	*F5000 McLaren M10B*	3rd
22 Jul	Watkins Glen 1,000 km	*Mirage M6*	3rd (with Carlos Pace)
1 Aug	German Grand Prix	*F1 Tecno PA123*	Rtd
10 Sept	Italian Grand Prix	*F1 Tecno PA123*	Did not qualify
24 Sept	Canadian Grand Prix	*F1 Tecno PA123*	Did not start
8 Oct	US Grand Prix	*F1 Tecno PA123*	Rtd
5 Nov	Jarama 2-hrs	*Osella-Abarth*	**1st**

1973

3-4 Feb	Daytona 24-hrs	*Mirage M6 300*	Rtd
25 March	Vallelunga 6-hrs	*Mirage M6 300*	Rtd
15 Apr	Dijon 1,000 km	*Mirage M6 300*	Rtd
6 May	Spa 1,000 km	*Mirage M6 300*	**1st** (with Mike Hailwood)
27 May	Nurburgring 1,000 km	*Mirage M6 300*	Rtd
9-10 Jun	Le Mans 24-hrs	*Mirage M6 300*	Rtd
24 Jun	Austrian 1,000 km	*Mirage M6 300*	5th (with Howden Ganley)
21 Jul	Watkins Glen 6-hrs	*Mirage M6 300*	4th (with Howden Ganley)
12 Aug	Mid Ohio Can-Am	*McLaren M8FP*	4th
23 Sept	Silverstone TT	*BMW CSL*	**1st** (with Harald Ertl)

1974	*14 Apr*	Salzburgring	*BMW CSL*	Rtd
	25 Apr	Monza 1,000 km	*Gulf GR7*	4th (with Mike Hailwood)
	5 May	Spa 1,000 km	*Gulf GR7*	2nd (with Mike Hailwood)
	19 May	Nurburgring 1,000 km	*Gulf GR7*	4th (with James Hunt and Vern Schuppan)
	9 Jun	Hockenheim	*F2 Surtees TS15X-BMW*	Rtd
	15-16 Jun	Le Mans 24-hrs	*Gulf GR7*	4th (with Mike Hailwood)
	23 Jun	Clermont Ferrand	*Osella PA2*	Rtd (fastest lap)
	30 Jun	Austrian 1,000 km	*Gulf GR7*	4th (with Mike Hailwood)
	14 Jul	Nurburgring 6-hrs	*BMW CSL*	
	20 Jul	British Grand Prix	*F1 Surtees TS16*	Did not qualify
	4 Aug	German Grand Prix	*F1 Surtees TS16*	11th
	15 Aug	Paul Ricard 1,000 km	*Gulf GR7*	3rd (with Jacky Ickx)
	18 Aug	Austrian Grand Prix	*F1 Surtees TS16*	Did not qualify
	8 Sept	Italian Grand Prix	*F1 Surtees TS16*	Did not qualify
	22 Sept	Canadian Grand Prix	*F1 Surtees TS16*	Did not qualify
	29 Sept	Brands Hatch 1,000 km	*Gulf GR7*	3rd (with David Hobbs)
	10 Nov	Kyalami 9-hrs	*Gulf GR7*	3rd (with David Hobbs)
1975	*23 Mar*	Mugello 1,000 km	*Alfa T33TT12*	4th (with Henri Pescarolo)
	6 Apr	Dijon 1,000 km	*Alfa T33TT12*	4th (with Henri Pescarolo)
	20 Apr	Monza 1,000 km	*Alfa T33TT12*	18th (with Henri Pescarolo)
	4 May	Spa 1,000 km	*Alfa T33TT12*	**1st** (with Henri Pescarolo)
	18 May	Enna-Pergusa	*Alfa T33TT12*	2nd (with Henri Pescarolo)
	14-15 Jun	Le Mans 24-hrs	*Mirage GR8*	**1st** (with Jacky Ickx)
	29 Jun	Austrian 1,000 km	*Alfa T33TT12*	**1st** (with Henri Pescarolo)
	12 Jul	Watkins Glen 6-hrs	*Alfa T33TT12*	**1st** (with Henri Pescarolo)
		Kyalami 9-hrs	*BMW CSL*	4th
1976	*30 May*	Nurburgring 1,000 km	*Porsche 935*	3rd (with Reinhardt Stenzel and Helmut Kelleners) and 10th with Stenzel, Kelleners and Gunther Steckkonig)
	12-13 Jun	Le Mans 24-hrs	*Mirage GR8*	5th (with Vern Schuppan)
	27 Jun	Austrian 1,000 km	*Porsche 935*	4th (with Vern Schuppan)
	19 Sept	Silverstone TT	*Jaguar XJC*	Rtd
	24 Oct	Brands Hatch GP	*F1 Penske PC3*	4th
	7 Nov	Brands Hatch Club	*F1 Penske PC3*	2nd

1977	*27 Mar*	Monza 4-hrs	*Jaguar XJC*	Rtd
	11 Apr	Oulton Park	*F1 Penske PC3*	**1st**
	24 Apr	Salzburgring	*Jaguar XJC*	Rtd
	8 May	Mugello	*Jaguar XJC*	Rtd
	15 May	Silverstone 6-hrs	*Porsche 935*	Rtd
	22 May	Enna-Pegusa	*Jaguar XJC*	Rtd
	29 May	Nurburgring 1,000 km	*Porsche 935*	Rtd
	5 Jun	Brno	*Jaguar XJC*	Rtd
	6 Jun	Thruxton	*F1 Penske PC3*	Rtd
	11-12 Jun	Le Mans 24-hrs	*Renault A442*	Rtd
	10 Jul	Nurburgring	*Jaguar XJC*	2nd (with Andy Rouse)
	24 Jul	Mallory Park	*F1 Penske PC3*	Rtd
	31 Jul	Donington Park	*F1 Penske PC3*	4th
	7 Aug	Zandvoort	*Jaguar XJC*	Rtd
	29 Aug	Brands Hatch	*F1 Penske PC3*	Rtd
	18 Sept	Silverstone TT	*Jaguar XJC*	4th, not running (with Andy Rouse)
	25 Sept	Zolder	*Jaguar XJC*	Rtd
		Spa 24-hrs	*BMW*	Rtd
		Avus	*Alfa Romeo TT33/12*	2nd
1978	*19 Mar*	Mugello 1,000 km	*BMW 320i*	3rd (with Dieter Quester)
	14 May	Silverstone 6-hrs	*Porsche 935*	Rtd
	28 May	Nurburgring 6-hrs	*Porsche 935*	Rtd
	10-11 Jun	Le Mans 24-hrs	*Alpine Renault A442B*	Rtd
	22-23 Jul	Spa 24-hrs	*Mazda RX7*	Rtd
	8 Oct	Bathurst	*Alfa Romeo*	Rtd
1979	*22 Apr*	Riverside	*Porsche 935*	3rd (with George Follmer and Brett Lunger)
	6 May	Silverstone 1,000 km	*Aston Martin*	13th (with David Preece)
	3 Jun	Nurburgring 1,000 km	*Porsche 935*	5th (with Rolf Stommelen and Volkert Merl)
	9/10 Jun	Le Mans 24-hrs	*Mirage M10*	Rtd (failed to complete last lap)
	15 Jul	Mid-Ohio	*BMW 320i turbo*	9th (with David Hobbs)
	1 Sept	Elkhart Lake	*BMW 320i turbo*	1st (with David Hobbs)
	30 Sept	Bathurst	*Alfa Romeo*	2nd in class
1980	*14/15 Jun*	Le Mans 24-hrs	*Porsche 924 Carrera GT*	13th (with Al Holbert)
	7 Sept	Vallelunga 6-hrs	*Porsche 908/3*	2nd (with Siegfried Brun)
		Bathurst	*Alfa Romeo GTV*	2nd in class

1981	*31 Jan/1 Feb*	Daytona 24-hrs	*Porsche 935*	2nd (with Bob Akin and Craig Siebert)
	21 Mar	Sebring 12-hrs	*Porsche 935*	Rtd
	10 May	Silverstone 6-hrs	*BMW M1*	2nd (with David Hobbs and Steve O'Rourke)
	13/14 Jun	Le Mans 24-hrs	*Porsche 936*	**1st** (with Jacky Ickx)
	18 Jul	Silverstone	*Porsche 917*	**1st**
		Spa 24-hrs	*BMW 530*	7th and 14th (drove two team entries)
	16 Aug	Mosport Park 1,000 km	*Porsche 934*	DNF
	23 Aug	Elkhart Lake	*Porsche 935*	Rtd
	30 Aug	Lumbermans 500, Mid-Ohio	*Porsche 935*	**1st** (with Rolf Stommelen)
	27 Sept	Brands Hatch 1,000 km	*BMW M1*	3rd (with Chris Craft)
	4 Oct	Bathurst	*Mazda RX7*	
		Kyalami 9-hrs	*Porsche 935*	3rd
1982	*30/31 Jan*	Daytona 24-hrs	*Porsche 935*	2nd (with Bob Akin and Craig Siebert)
	20 Mar	Sebring 12-hrs	*Porsche 935*	12th (with Bob Akin and Craig Siebert)
	25 Apr	Riverside 6-hrs	*Porsche 935*	4th (with Bob Akin and Craig Siebert
	16 May	Silverstone 1,000 km	*Porsche 956*	2nd (with Jacky Ickx)
	19/20 Jun	Le Mans 24-hrs	*Porsche 956*	**1st** (with Jacky Ickx)
	15 Aug	Mosport Park	*Porsche 935*	4th (with Bob Akin)
	22 Aug	Elkhart Lake	*Porsche 935*	Rtd
	5 Sept	Spa, 1,000 km	*Porsche 956*	2nd (with Vern Schuppan)
	12 Sept	Road Atlanta	*Porsche 935*	7th (with Bob Akin)
	26 Sept	Pocono	*Porsche 935*	Rtd
	3 Oct	Fuji 1,000 km	*Porsche 956*	Rtd
	17 Oct	Brands Hatch 1,000 km	*Porsche 956*	**1st** (with Jacky Ickx)
	6 Nov	Kyalami 9-hrs	*Porsche 956*	2nd (with Vern Schuppan)
	28 Nov	Daytona 3-hrs	*Porsche 935*	3rd (with Randy Lanier)
1983	*27 Feb*	GP of Miami	*Porsche 935*	Rtd
	19 Mar	Sebring 12-hrs	*Porsche 935*	Rtd
	10 Apr	Monza 1,000 km	*Porsche 956*	7th (with Al Holbert)
	24 Apr	Riverside	*Porsche 935*	**1st** (with David Hobbs and John Fitzpatrick)
	8 May	Silverstone 1,000 km	*Porsche 956*	**1st** (with Stefan Bellof)
	29 May	Nurburgring 1,000 km	*Porsche 956*	Rtd
	18/19 June	Le Mans 24-hrs	*Porsche 956*	2nd (with Jacky Ickx)
	4 Sept	Spa 1,000 km	*Porsche 956*	2nd (with Stefan Bellof)
	18 Sept	Brands Hatch 1,000 km	*Porsche 956*	3rd (with Stefan Bellof)
	2 Oct	Fuji 1,000 km	*Porsche 956*	**1st** (with Stefan Bellof)
	16 Oct	Imola 1,000 km	*Porsche 956*	4th (with Jonathan Palmer)

23 Oct	Mugello 1,000 km	*Porsche 956*	3rd (with Jonathan Palmer and Henri Toivonen)
10 Dec	Kyalami 1,000 km	*Porsche 956*	**1st** (with Stefan Bellof)

1984

4/5 Feb	Daytona 24-hrs	*Porsche 935*	2nd (with Bob Wollek and A. J. Foyt)
24 Mar	Sebring 12-hrs	*Porsche 935*	3rd (with Bob Wollek and A. J. Foyt)
8 Apr	Road Atlanta	*Porsche 935*	Rtd
23 Apr	Monza 1,000 km	*Porsche 956*	**1st** (with Stefan Bellof)
29 Apr	Riverside	*Porsche 962*	2nd (with Al Holbert)
6 May	Laguna Seca	*Porsche 962*	8th
13 May	Silverstone 1,000 km	*Porsche 956*	10th (with Stefan Bellof)
20 May	Charlotte	*Porsche 962*	Rtd
10 June	Lumbermans 500, Mid-Ohio	*Porsche 956*	**1st** (with Al Holbert)
16 June	Brooklyn, Michigan, IROC	*Chevy Camaro*	10th
7 Jul	Cleveland, Ohio, IROC	*Chevy Camaro*	2nd
8 July	Watkins Glen Double 3hr	*Porsche 962*	**1st** (with Al Holbert and Jim Adams)
15 July	Nurburgring 1,000 km	*Porsche 956*	**1st** (with Stefan Bellof)
28 Jul	Alabama, IROC	*Chevy Camaro*	9th
29 July	Portland	*Porsche 962*	3rd (with Al Holbert)
5 Aug	Mosport Park 1,000 km	*Porsche 956*	4th (with Stefan Bellof)
11 Aug	Brooklyn, Michigan, IROC	*Chevy Camaro*	8th
26 Aug	Elkhart Lake	*Porsche 962*	**1st** (with Al Holbert)
2 Sept	Spa 1,000 km	*Porsche 956*	**1st** (with Stefan Bellof)
9 Sept	Pocono 500 km	*Porsche 962*	**1st** (with Al Holbert)
16 Sept	Michigan 500 km	*Porsche 962*	9th (with Al Holbert)
23 Sept	Brands Hatch F2	*March 842-BMW*	9th
25 Nov	Daytona 3-hrs	*Porsche 962*	**1st** (with Al Holbert)
2 Dec	Sandown Park 1,000 km	*Porsche 956*	**1st** (with Stefan Bellof)

1985

2/3 Feb	Daytona 24-hrs	*Porsche 962*	2nd (with Al Holbert and Al Unser Jnr)
15 Feb	IROC Daytona	*Chevy Camaro*	4th
24 Feb	GP of Miami	*Porsche 962*	**1st** (with Al Holbert)
23 March	Sebring 12-hrs	*Porsche 962*	2nd (with Al Holbert and Al Unser Jnr)
14 Apr	Mugello 6-hrs	*Porsche 962*	Disqualified
28 Apr	Monza 1,000 km	*Porsche 956*	2nd (with Hans Stuck)
12 May	Silverstone 1,000 km	*Porsche 956/962*	2nd (with Hans Stuck)
19 May	Charlotte	*Porsche 962*	**1st** (with Al Holbert)
8 Jun	Mid-Ohio IROC	*Chevy Camaro*	5th
9 Jun	Lumbermans 500, Mid-Ohio	*Porsche 962*	**1st** (with Al Holbert)
15/16 Jun	Le Mans 24-hrs	*Porsche 962*	3rd (with Hans Stuck)
7 July	Watkins Glen 3-hrs	*Porsche 962*	**1st** (with Al Holbert)
14 July	Hockenheim 1,000 km	*Porsche 962*	**1st** (with Hans Stuck)
27 July	IROC Talladega	*Chevy Camaro*	Rained off

28 July	Portland 3-hrs	*Porsche 962*	Rtd
4 Aug	Sears Point	*Porsche 962*	7th (with Al Holbert)
10 Aug	Michigan IROC	*Chevy Camaro*	6th
11 Aug	Mosport Park 1,000 km	*Porsche 962*	**1st** (with Hans Stuck)
25 Aug	Elkhart Lake	*Porsche 962*	Rtd
1 Sept	Spa 1,000 km	*Porsche 962*	2nd (with Hans Stuck)
8 Sept	Pocono 500 km	*Porsche 962*	**1st** (with Al Holbert)
22 Sept	Brands Hatch 1,000 km	*Porsche 962*	**1st** (with Hans Stuck)
29 Sept	Watkins Glen 500 km	*Porsche 962*	**1st** (with Al Holbert)
6 Oct	Fuji 1,000 km	*Porsche 962*	Withdrawn
1 Dec	Selangor 800 km	*Porsche 962*	Rtd

1986

1/2 Feb	Daytona 24-hrs	*Porsche 962*	**1st** (with Al Holbert and Al Unser Jnr)
2 Mar	GP of Miami	*Porsche 962*	6th (with Al Holbert)
22 Mar	Sebring 12-hrs	*Porsche 962*	3rd (with Al Holbert and Al Unser Jnr)
6 Apr	Road Atlanta	*Porsche 962*	3rd (with Al Holbert)
20 Apr	Monza 1,000 km	*Porsche 962*	**1st** (with Hans Stuck)
27 Apr	Los Angeles GP, Riverside	*Porsche 962*	Rtd
5 May	Silverstone 1,000 km	*Porsche 962*	2nd (with Hans Stuck)
18 May	Charlotte	*Porsche 962*	Rtd
26 May	Lime Rock	*Porsche 962*	4th
31 May/ 1 Jun	Le Mans 24-hrs	*Porsche 962*	**1st** (with Hans Stuck and Al Holbert)
8 Jun	Mid-Ohio	*Porsche 962*	**1st** (with Al Holbert)
15 Jun	Hockenheim	*Porsche 962*	3rd
22 Jun	Palm Beach 3-hrs	*Porsche 962*	4th (with Al Holbert)
29 Jun	200 von Nurnberg	*Porsche 962*	11th
6 July	Watkins Glen 500 km	*Porsche 962*	**1st** (with Al Holbert)
20 July	Brands Hatch 1,000 km	*Porsche 956*	2nd (with Hans Stuck and Klaus Ludwig)
27 July	Portland	*Porsche 962*	7th
3 Aug	Sears Point 300 km	*Porsche 962*	2nd (with Al Holbert)
24 Aug	Nurburgring 1,000 km	*Porsche 962*	Rtd
14 Sept	Spa 1,000 km	*Porsche 962*	3rd (with Hans Stuck)
21 Sept	Watkins Glen 500 km	*Porsche 962*	2nd (with Al Holbert)
5 Oct	Fuji 1,000 km	*Porsche 962*	Rtd
26 Oct	Daytona 3-hrs	*Porsche 962*	6th (with Al Holbert)

1987

31 Jan/1 Feb	Daytona 24-hours	*Porsche 962*	**1st** (with Al Holbert, Chip Robinson, Al Unser Jnr.
13 Feb	Daytona IROC	*Chevy Camaro*	Rtd
1 Mar	GP of Miami	*Porsche 962*	4th (with Chip Robinson)
22 Mar	GP Fortuna, Jarama	*Porsche 962*	2nd (with Hans Stuck)
29 Mar	Jerez 1,000 km	*Porsche 962*	3rd (with Hans Stuck)
12 Apr	Monza 1,000 km	*Porsche 962*	2nd (with Hans Stuck)
10 May	Silverstone 1,000 km	*Porsche 962*	3rd (with Hans Stuck)

6 Jun	Mid Ohio 500 km	*Porsche 962*	Rtd
13/14 Jun	Le Mans 24-hrs	*Porsche 962*	**1st** (with Hans Stuck and Al Holbert)
21 Jun	3-hrs of Palm Beach	*Porsche 962*	2nd (with Chip Robinson)
28 Jun	200 Von Nurnberg	*Porsche 962*	Rtd
5 Jul	Watkins Glen 500 km	*Porsche 962*	Rtd
26 Jul	Brands Hatch 1,000 km	*Porsche 962*	4th (with Hans Stuck)
1 Aug	IROC Michigan	*Chevy Camaro*	7th
8 Aug	IROC Watkins Glen	*Chevy Camaro*	11th
16 Aug	Elkhart Lake, 500 km	*Porsche 962*	4th
30 Aug	Nurburgring 1,000 km	*Porsche 962*	2nd (with Hans Stuck)
6 Sept	San Antonio 3-hrs	*Porsche 962*	**1st** (with Chip Robinson and Al Holbert)
13 Sept	Spa 1,000 km	*Porsche 962*	5th (with Hans Stuck and Bob Wollek)
27 Sept	Fuji 1,000 km	*Porsche 962*	6th (with Geoff Brabham)
4 Oct	Columbus 500 km	*Porsche 962*	4th (with Chip Robinson)
25 Oct	GP of S. California	*Porsche 962*	Rtd
1988 *30/31 Jan*	Daytona 24-hrs	*Porsche 962C*	Rtd

Awards and achievements

World Sports Car Champion 1985 and 1986
Le Mans winner 1975, 1981, 1982, 1986 and 1987
BRDC Gold Star 1984, 1985, 1986 and 1987
RAC Plaque d'Honneur 1985
Guild of Motoring Writers Driver of the Year 1982 and 1985
Awarded MBE in 1986 for services to motor racing

Index